In Touch with the Word

with the

Lectionary-Based
Prayer Reflections

In Touch with the Word

Lectionary-Based Prayer Reflections

Cycle C for Ordinary Time

Lisa-Marie Calderone-Stewart

Saint Mary's Press
Christian Brothers Publications
Winona, Minnesota

- Thank-you, Fr. Bob Stamschror, for your constant affirmation and guidance in this project and in all the projects we envision and accomplish together. It is a joy to work with you.
- Thank-you, Ralph, for the love and care you give me every day, as well as the technical assistance I need whenever our computer doesn't understand what I want it to do.
- Thank-you, Bishop Ken Untener. You have had a major influence on my spiritual formation, my ministry, and my life.

 Genuine recycled paper with 10% post-consumer waste. Printed with soy-based ink.

The publishing team for this book included Robert P. Stamschror, development editor; Laurie A. Berg, copy editor; Barbara Bartelson, production editor and typesetter; Stephan Nagel and Kent Linder, cover designers; Maurine R. Twait, art director; prepress, printing, and binding by the graphics division of Saint Mary's Press.

The acknowledgments continue on page 132.

Printed in the United States of America

Printing: 9 8 7 6 5 4 3 2 1

Year: 2005 04 03 02 01 00 99 98 97

ISBN 0-88489-513-0, paper
ISBN 0-88489-533-5, spiral

I dedicate this book to my uncle,
Philip J. Calderone, SJ,
who teaches seminary at the Loyola House of Studies
in Manila, Philippines.

When I was little, I thought they named the country
after you!
What a blessing that our physical distance never
got in the way of our emotional and spiritual
closeness.
I love you and I miss you.

Contents

Introduction 9

Ordinary Time of the Year

Introduction

Did you ever go to Mass on Sunday, listen to the Scripture readings, and then promptly forget what they were all about or how your life relates to their message? Does this sound familiar? Even though you may have listened to a homilist who connected the word with you and challenged you at that time, what about the week before the Sunday Scriptures or the week after? How can you anticipate and prepare for the word? How can you stay in touch with the word that was heard?

This book is a resource designed to do just that—to help you prepare for the Sunday Scripture readings and to help you stay in touch with the word.

Using This Book

Using *In Touch with the Word* is a simple procedure. First, decide which Sunday's readings you are going to share. If it is Friday afternoon, you might want to reflect on the readings for the next Sunday so you can be more prepared for the upcoming liturgy. If it is Monday morning, you might want to remember the readings you heard on Sunday so you can stay in touch with that word the rest of the week. Next, turn to the page for the Sunday you have in mind. There you will find reflections, questions, and a prayer based on that Sunday's readings.

The Sunday Scripture Readings

The Scripture readings for each Sunday of the year are found in a book called a lectionary. The Sunday readings follow a three-year, A-B-C cycle that continues to repeat itself. The readings in the A cycle highlight the Gospel of Matthew. The readings in the B cycle highlight the Gospel of Mark. The readings in the C cycle highlight the Gospel of Luke. (If you are wondering about the Gospel of John, don't be concerned. His readings are woven throughout all three years on special days that seem to need that "John" touch.)

The church calendar year consists of the seasons of Advent and Christmas, Lent and Easter, plus Ordinary Time. This book covers Ordinary Time, C cycle only. (The Sundays of B and A cycle in Ordinary Time, and the Sundays of the Advent, Christmas, Lent, and Easter seasons will be found in other volumes of this series.) Most Sundays have three sets of readings, one for each cycle. But in this book you will only find the readings for the C cycle. The dates for each Sunday in the C cycle are given for the next several years.

You will note that the Scripture readings are not reprinted in this book. It would make the book too big and too expensive. You will need either a lectionary or a Bible to read one or more of the Scripture readings as part of the prayer reflection. However, a capsulated version of each Scripture reading is provided.

One of the three Scripture readings listed with each Sunday has an open bullet (○) next to it. This indicates which reading will be most focused on in the reflection and which one you might want to read as part of the reflection.

Theme

A summary of a central theme of the readings is also offered. You may want to use it to set a context for the reflection questions that will initiate sharing of and reflecting on the word.

Reflections

The reflection questions for each Sunday address audiences in three categories: adults, teenagers, and children. However, feel free to cross categories in the use of the questions whenever it is appropriate.

Focusing Object

For each set of readings, you will find a suggested focusing object. Using a focusing object in these prayer reflections is not mandatory, but it is helpful, especially with teenagers and children. It is a visual, hands-on reminder of the readings and their message. For example, anticipating or recalling the meaning of the passage about our relationship with Jesus being like a vine and its branches is much easier and more vivid if a plant with a stem and branches is present when reflecting on the reading of that passage.

The focusing object is handy for facilitating the prayer reflection and sharing. For example, after the Scripture reading is proclaimed, the facilitator asks one of the reflection questions for everyone to think about and share their thoughts. Then the facilitator picks up the focusing object and begins the sharing. When finished, the facilitator passes the object to the next person who is ready to share.

The focusing object can be passed around a circle, so everyone knows when their turn is coming, or it can be passed randomly as people become ready to share. A large group does better sitting in a circle and passing the object around in order. In a small group—one that fits around a table where everyone can reach the middle—anyone who is ready can pick up the object, share, and replace it for the next person who is ready to take a turn. Also, using the object makes it obvious when a person's turn has ended—no one has to guess. If someone just wants to offer a one-word response, or even remain silent, the focusing object is simply handed to the next person.

The focusing object is more than a reminder or a turn-designator. It is also an effective way to reduce the self-conscious feeling many people get when they are expected to share with a group of their peers. Persons handling an object and looking at it tend to relax and forget that a roomful of people is watching them. People who are relaxed and comfortable do a better job of sharing. This is true of adults, teenagers, and children!

After everyone has had a chance to share, the object comes back to the facilitator, who ends with the "Closing" or any other words she or he feels would be appropriate. The focusing object can stay on a kitchen table or a classroom shelf all week, acting as a reminder of God's word and the people's response.

Closing

A closing is provided for each prayer reflection. It consists of a poem or reading that ends the reflections with an inspirational touch. You will notice that the closings come from a variety of cultures and each culture adds a rich spiritual tradition to the prayer reflections.

Indexes

Each Sunday's prayer session is indexed by focusing object and by theme in the back of this book.

Settings

Parish

Parish staffs, councils, and committees usually want to start their meetings with some type of prayer. Prayer based on Sunday's readings is a great way to help the group relate to the parish liturgy, connect with the message of the Sunday readings, and start the meeting off on a spiritual plane.

Homilists can benefit from this resource by looking at the message through the eyes of adults, teenagers, and children. This can provide a springboard for the type of insights needed to be pastoral, effective, and challenging to the assembly of mixed ages that typically gathers each Sunday. (Actually sharing the reflection questions with adults, teenagers, and children and listening to their responses each week provides even better feedback for a homilist!)

Liturgy planning groups will find this book helpful. Members with different degrees of liturgical experience and understanding can read the theme summaries, share the questions, and get a feel for the flow of the Scriptures. The suggested focusing object can also remind the group to investigate the possibilities of symbolism in the physical environment of the worship space.

Prayer groups and small Christian communities will find *In Touch with the Word* very helpful, especially if the groups include families with children of different ages.

Youth Groupings

Youth ministers will find the prayer reflections in this book a simple way to prepare a youth group or team for the readings they will hear the following Sunday or feast day and to help them stay in touch with the readings they heard the previous Sunday. At the same time, the reflections call attention to the major seasons of the church year. The prayer process in the reflection works equally well with junior high teens or high school teens.

Parish religious education teachers and catechists meeting with a class once a week can use this resource to relate to the Sunday and feast day readings. Sending a note home each week encouraging parents to discuss the readings with their children at the dinner table or at bedtime, perhaps with a similar focusing object, is a good way to weave a family connection into a parish religious education program.

Religion teachers in Catholic schools looking for a way to connect students with their parish community will value this resource. Anticipating or recalling the Scriptures read at the parish liturgies will help students stay in touch with their parish community.

Families

Busy families will find that using *In Touch with the Word* at home is a great way to make liturgical worship more relevant for their teenagers or younger children. Using the prayer reflections does not take long and is easy to do. Best of all, it helps the family as a whole connect with what is said at Mass and remember it throughout the week. Parents may find their teenagers more likely to share prayer if they are doing it "for the sake of their younger brothers and sisters" than if they think they are doing it for themselves!

Parishes with family-based programming can use this resource in several ways. If the parish supplies families with resources to be used at home, every family can receive a copy of *In Touch with the Word* to use on their own. If families gather regularly at the parish for a scheduled activity, the sharing process can be incorporated with the program. If family groups meet in cells or units, they can be provided with copies of this book and suggestions for how it can be used in the context of their meeting.

Whether you work with adults, teenagers, or children in a parish, school, or home setting, you will find that being in touch with the word is easy with *In Touch with the Word*.

Trinity Sunday

7 June 1998
10 June 2001
6 June 2004

The Trinity

Scripture

- *Proverbs 8:22–31.* Wisdom delights that she was there when our almighty Creator God brought forth the mountains, the fields, and the seas.
- *Romans 5:1–5.* We are at peace with our Creator, we are graced through Jesus our Redeemer, and our hope in the Holy Spirit will not leave us disappointed.
- *John 16:12–15.* The Holy Spirit gives glory to Jesus. The Spirit will declare the truth that is God's, and we will know that the Spirit comes from God.

Theme

There is a special relationship between God our Creator, Jesus our Redeemer, and their Holy and Divine Spirit. One of the greatest mysteries of our faith is the Trinity—the one God that is, at the same time, three distinct persons—all affecting our life, and all entities with whom we can relate.

We are part of and share in the delight of God the Creator's creation and the grace that Jesus won for us. We can also share in the truth that the Spirit brings to us.

Focusing Object
shamrock, a clover with three leaves

Reflections

The shamrock is an ancient symbol of the Trinity, one plant with three leaves whose life juices are intermingled. God exists as love, as a community of three persons. Like the Trinity, we are called to exist as a community of loving persons.

- Which is harder for you to understand and believe: that one God exists as a community of divine persons, or that we are one human family called to exist as a community of loving persons?
- Who are the people in your life who form the closest community of love and support for you?
- Who are some people in your life that you would rather not exist in such "close community" with? Why? How do you deal with this reality?

The Spirit brings truth. It is often said that the Holy Spirit is the person of God that dwells within us and acts as our conscience, guiding us toward doing what is right and just. Following the way of the Spirit is the main message of every Gospel.

- Has the Holy Spirit ever brought you a painful truth you had to face?
- Has the Holy Spirit ever led you to a difficult decision you needed to make?
- Do you think your life is a good attempt at living out the main message of the Gospels? Why or why not?

For Teenagers

Saint Patrick is famous for making the shamrock a handy tool to illustrate the Blessed Trinity: one plant, three leaves that are all connected and united—symbolizing the one God, three persons that are all connected and united.

- Sometimes close relationships are also compared to the Trinity: the person you love, the person who loves you, and God. If God is a part of your relationship, it's hard to think of the two of you without the power, joy, and courage that God brings. Do you have any relationships like that? What are they like?

- A family, a team, or a close group of friends can also form a community of love that is similar to the Trinity—several persons that are connected and united in a very special way. Do you belong to any such group? If so, what makes it special?
- The Holy Spirit brings the truth of God. Sometimes in our life we are running away from a truth, or trying to ignore or avoid it. What basic truth in your life do you think God wants you to be more aware of?
- Sometimes in our life, when we have done something wrong or when we are about to do something wrong, the Spirit of God speaks to us through our conscience. Have you ever thought about doing something, until that voice inside you called you to do something else? What happened?
- The main message of every Gospel is to know the way of the Spirit and to follow the way of the Spirit. How easy is it to live your life that way? How is living your life that way similar to preaching the Gospel?

For Children

Even though we can't see God, we know that the shamrock is like God. The shamrock is one plant that has three leaves, and we believe that our one God is three persons.

- God, the Creator, created the whole earth and sky, and all the animals and people who live here. Look outside, and tell about something God created.
- Jesus is God. Jesus lived here on earth a long time ago. Jesus told wonderful stories and healed people who were sick. Can you think of a story you have heard about Jesus?
- The Holy Spirit is God. The Holy Spirit lives inside of us and helps us feel happy whenever we do something good. When we do something wrong, the Holy Spirit helps us feel sad inside, so we know that what we did was wrong.
- Did you ever feel the Holy Spirit helping you feel happy or sad inside? What happened?

Closing

A part of the act of baptism in the Church of India is for the candidates to place their own hand on their head and say, "Woe to me if I preach not the Gospel." —E. Paul Hovey

(Action 2000: C Cycle)

Feast of the Body and Blood of Christ

14 June 1998
17 June 2001
13 June 2004

The Body and Blood of Jesus

Scripture

- *Genesis 14:18–20.* Melchizedek brings forth bread and wine and blesses Abraham as a sign that God highly favors Abraham.
- *1 Corinthians 11:23–26.* Jesus broke bread, poured wine, blessed it, and asked his disciples to eat and drink. He told them, "Do this in memory of me."
- *Luke 9:11–17.* The crowd of over five thousand was hungry, and Jesus fed them all with the five loaves and two fish the Apostles brought forth.

Theme

Meals can be special times. We celebrate with meals and we can create memories with meals. The blessing of Melchizedek is echoed in the blessing of Jesus at his last supper with his disciples. The great feeding of the crowd of five thousand is recorded in each of the four Gospels; an additional story of Jesus feeding a crowd of four thousand is told in Matthew's and Mark's Gospels. These are meals to remember!

The images that build the theme call our attention to the many ways that Jesus feeds our hungers, and the importance of sharing food with all who are hungry.

Focusing Object
An empty cup and dish

Reflections

For Adults

An ancient African custom teaches that if a person feeds you, teaches you, or helps you in any way, then you are to speak highly of that person. Your words of praise keep alive the spirit of that person's goodness so that it can continue to flow. Speaking well of the person who has helped you is expected to continue on, even if that person later wrongs you, because goodness outlives evil.

- Who are the people who fed you, taught you, and helped you? Do you still speak well of them, or have you forgotten their goodness to you?
- Who has given us more than God has? How well and how often do you speak of God and God's blessings in your life?

When we gather as church, it is not only to feed our body, but also to feed our spirit.

- How are we fed by our faith community?
- How do we feed others in our faith community?

For Teenagers

An ancient African custom teaches that if a person feeds you, teaches you, or helps you in any way, then you are to speak highly of that person. Your words of praise keep alive the spirit of that person's goodness, so that it can continue to flow.

Criticizing teachers, parents, or coaches we dislike or disagree with is an easy practice to fall into. But they are usually the ones who care the most about us and who are trying to help us become better people.

- What are some good things you can say about your parents, teachers, or coaches?
- What are some good things your parents, teachers, or coaches could say about you?

When Jesus had his last meal with his closest friends, he asked them to remember him when sharing this special meal together.

- When you are at Eucharist, eating that special meal of Jesus' body and blood, how do you remember Jesus? What do you think about? Is your mind on Jesus, or are your thoughts usually floating somewhere else?

For Children

You probably know that when people go to church and eat the Communion bread, they are not eating just ordinary bread. They are actually receiving Jesus into their body. The same thing happens when they drink the Communion wine. It is a very special, very holy meal.
- If you have received your first Communion already, what was it like? Can you remember what that day was like for you and your family?
- If you haven't received your first Communion yet, when do you think it will happen? How old will you be? What do you think it will be like?

Closing

If you eat well, you must speak well. —A Yoruba proverb

(Acts of Faith)

Second Sunday of the Year

Jesus Turns Water into Wine

Scripture

- *Isaiah 62:1–5.* Almighty God rejoices in each of us the way a bridegroom and bride rejoice in each other.
- *1 Corinthians 12:4–11.* Each of us is blessed with different gifts, but all our gifts come from the same Spirit of God.
- *John 2:1–12.* When the hosts run out of wine at a wedding in Cana, Mary encourages Jesus to do something about it.

Theme

There is something wonderful about a union—everyone loves a good wedding story where the two individuals promise to become one flesh, one entity. Isaiah reminds us that God loves us like a bride and groom love each other.

But we need to remember that it is the individuality of each separate person that makes each union so enriching. When different gifts from the same Spirit come together and are allowed to grow and to be shared—in a marriage, a friendship, a business partnership, or in a parent-child relationship like Jesus and Mary's—the union is blessed and is made fuller.

Focusing Object
Six glasses or jars of water

Reflections

For Adults

The freedom of each person to choose to unite is crucial for a healthy union. Two people who can manage well alone but choose to be together will have a stronger relationship than two people who feel pressured to be together because they feel inadequate when they are apart. In fact, a personal bond is only possible when it is freely chosen.

• Think of one of your closer relationships. Are you deliberately choosing to stay in this relationship? Have you ever felt "trapped" and wanted to get out? Have you ever felt that you have no other option but to stay?

The backdrop of this first miracle of Jesus is a wedding—a symbol of unity. Yet the focus of the story is not the bride and groom's relationship, but Mary's relationship with Jesus—another symbol of unity. Just as differences enrich a marriage, differences enriched Jesus and Mary's relationship.

It was not Jesus' idea to create more wine for the wedding couple. And yet Mary did not coerce him, either. She told him of their predicament and let him decide what to do.

• When was a time that you took action in a similar situation—not because you were coerced or manipulated, but because someone you respected pointed out a possible opportunity for you? What was the outcome?

Mary did not tell Jesus what to do, but she knew him well enough to know that he would probably choose to help. Wanting to make the way easier for him, she took the liberty of speaking with the waiters and encouraging them to do whatever Jesus asked of them.

- When have you "paved the way" for someone else to offer their talents and skills in resolving a situation, not knowing exactly what that person might do? What happened?

For Teenagers

Jesus isn't interested in listening to his mother at first. But he seems to rethink the situation. After some thought, he goes ahead and does something that she probably would approve of.

- When was a time that your mother or father or some older relative was trying to get you to consider an option, and you just didn't want to go along with their idea? But later, when you thought about it, you came to understand his or her point of view and did what he or she wanted you to do? How did it work out?

Jesus' first miracle wasn't very splashy. Most people didn't even know what had happened. The waiters kept it low-key and didn't make a big deal about the wine that had just been water in the six jars only moments before. Mary doesn't seem to say anything more about it, and Jesus also plays it cool. Yet the needs were met—without a lot of fuss.

- When was a time that you took matters into your own hands to take care of a pressing need, but did it in a very low-key way?
- Was there a kind of delight to such a secret act of kindness—a kind of self-satisfaction that comes from inside? Why is that?

For Children

Mary and Jesus were at a party for two people who had just been married. A lot of people were still there at the party, but the hosts ran out of wine. This was a problem for the wedding couple because they wanted all their party guests to share special food and drink. Mary knew that Jesus could somehow take care of this problem, so she told Jesus that they had run out of wine.

- How would you feel if you had some of your friends come to your house for a birthday party and your parents told you that they had run out of things to drink?
- What would your party be like without party punch or milk or something good to drink? Would you want your friends to drink only water? Why or why not?

Jesus wasn't sure he wanted to do anything at first, but then he told the waiters to fill six big jars with water. Then as soon as they took a cup of the water over to the waiter in charge, it wasn't water anymore! It had turned into wine! And it was the best wine anyone had ever had. But the waiters didn't tell anyone where it had come from. Neither did Jesus or Mary.

- What would your party be like if one of your friends poured water into six cups, and then when you went to drink it, it wasn't water anymore at all, but party punch—the best party punch you had ever had?
- What would you say to your friend? What would you tell your parents? Would you keep it a secret or would you want to tell everyone? Why?

Closing

As I have grown, . . . I have come to realize that it is the separateness of the partners that enriches the union.

(The Road Less Traveled)

Third Sunday of the Year

25 January 1998
21 January 2001
25 January 2004

Many Members, One Body

Scripture

- *Nehemiah 8:2–4,5–6,8–10.* Ezra reads from the scroll and tells the people that today is a holy day for rejoicing.
- *1 Corinthians 12:12–30.* The body has many different members that do different things, but all are needed for the entire body to work well.
- *Luke 1:1–4; 4:14–21.* Jesus reads from the scroll and tells the people that today is a special day, for the Scriptures are being fulfilled in their hearing.

Theme

Every member of the body is important. The hand is not better than the foot, and the eye is not more important than the ear. The hand would look silly all by itself without the rest of the body, and so would the eye, foot, or ear.

Every person in a group is also important. Some have the job of reading from the scroll, and some have the job of responding. The reader would look pretty silly all alone, proclaiming the truth from the holy book, if no one was there to hear the words and rejoice.

Focusing Object

A picture of a person—one that shows the whole body

Reflections

In our culture it is a common perception that the only ones who count are the ones in charge. Many people strive to climb the ladder of success so that they in turn will be able to look down on the folks who are still below, on the bottom rungs.

- Do I, in any way, contribute to this ladder point of view?
- How do I work against the ladder point of view so that everyone is perceived as being important?
- Do I somehow "look up to" those who are "ahead of me" in my line of work?
- Do I "look down upon" those who are "behind me"? How do I know who is ahead of or behind me? Or do I avoid this type of categorizing?
- Saint Paul talks of the importance of every member of the human body. Have you ever stubbed your little toe? Isn't it amazing how this tiny part of your body that you hardly ever notice can disturb every other body part when it hurts? How does this analogy relate to a society of people?
- When the "least important" member of society is hurting or suffering, do you suffer? Do you care? Are you even aware of that suffering? What can you do to become more aware of that pain and to play a part in easing it?

Saint Paul reminds us that every member of a group or body is important.

- At your school, is one group of students perceived as being "more important" than the others? If so, why is that? Who are they—the smartest students? the best athletes? the most attractive looking males and females? the teens with the most money?
- Is it true that these students are any more important than the others? Where does this false perception come from?

The study of biology can show us how the different parts of our body work together. The heart pumps the blood around, the lungs clean out the blood, the stomach and intestines process the food that fuels the body, the eyes and ears help direct the way the feet walk and the hands move. If something happens to one leg, the other leg and arms grow stronger, often with the help of crutches, in an effort to keep the body going. If the skin is bruised or broken, blood rushes to cleanse and clot in the area. Even if the eyesight is poor, the ears and nose cooperate in order to keep a pair of glasses in place!

- Is this the way your school or community functions? Do people generally watch out for one another when someone is weakened or hurt or in need of help? If so, how? If not, why not?
- Is this the way your family works? Do some family members come to the aid of others in need? If so, how? If not, why not?

For Children

God made your body with many different parts so that it can do lots of wonderful things!

- What do your eyes like to look at?
- What do your ears like to listen to?
- Where do your feet like to walk to?
- What does your nose like to smell?
- What does your mouth like to taste and swallow?
- What do your hands like to play with?

Closing

It is astounding . . . how much energy the body is capable of pouring out and then replenishing. That is a magical act, because you never really understand where all that energy comes from.
—Robert Bly

(The Promise of a New Day)

Fourth Sunday of the Year

1 February 1998
28 January 2001
1 February 2004

The Greatest
of These
Is Love

Scripture

- *Jeremiah 1:4–5,17–19.* Yahweh knows each of us in the womb before we are even born. Yahweh promises to be with Jeremiah—and with us.
- *1 Corinthians 12:31—13:13.* The greatest of all the virtues is the virtue of love.
- *Luke 4:21–30.* Jesus sadly admits that prophets are not honored in their own country.

Theme

Love is the most important virtue there is. Without love, nothing matters. With love, everything matters. Love brings courage, support, strength, and even miracles. Jeremiah could do anything, because he was assured of God's love. Jesus could do very little when he felt no love from the people.

Focusing Object

A picture or sculpture of a heart

Reflections

For Adults

Real love endures, believes, and hopes. Love is power.

- When has love empowered you to do something you did not think you were capable of doing? What happened?

- What is your definition of love?
- What is one of the greatest obstacles to love in your life?

For Teenagers

Love empowered Jeremiah. Lack of love stopped Jesus in his tracks.
- When has love empowered you to do something you didn't think you could do?
- When did a lack of love and support stop you in your tracks?

Saint Paul was writing about love. His words in First Corinthians are almost poetic.
- What modern song do you think captures the essence of what love is all about? How so?

For Children

Love is the most important thing there is. God loves you, and so do many other people.
- Can you tell when a person really loves you?
- When you want to show someone that you love them, what do you do?
- What are some of the ways you can tell that God loves you?
- Why do you think God put love into the world?

Closing

Our hearts are the wrapping which preserve God's word, we need no more. —The Koran, Sura 4:155

(Acts of Faith)

Fifth Sunday of the Year

8 February 1998
4 February 2001
8 February 2004

Fishers of Men and Women

Scripture

- *Isaiah 6:1–2,3–8.* Isaiah is afraid to serve God because of his sinfulness. He is assured that he is worthy to serve.
- *1 Corinthians 15:1–11.* Paul says that he is the least of all the Apostles.
- *Luke 5:1–11.* After seeing the miraculous catch of fish at Jesus' command, Peter tells Jesus to leave him, for he is a sinful man.

Theme

Sins and faults abound! Isaiah, Paul, and Peter—all great people—were also sinners. So are you and so am I. Their sinfulness affected their ability to believe in themselves and to think themselves worthy to serve God's purpose. But actually, because every human is imperfect and flawed, every human is a sinner. We are each equally "unfit to serve." That means we are also equally "fit to serve."

Not to worry! Jesus showed us that we need not be perfect. God can weave great things out of all of us, even though we are sinners.

Focusing Object

A fish

Reflections

Peter is overwhelmed with shame over his sins, once he realizes the miracle worker Jesus is. He is so filled with shame that he tells Jesus to leave him. But Jesus tells him to not be afraid. Even if he isn't such a great catcher of fish, he can take a shot at being a catcher of men and women. Jesus is willing to take him as he is.

- Have you ever been overwhelmed at your inadequacy?
- Have you ever been completely shamed over an action you committed? How did you get over it? Who reached out and told you to not be afraid?

We all have faults. But that is not an excuse to continue sinning without remorse or accountability. It is our job to always struggle to improve ourselves, and to become less sinful and more saintly.

- How do you view self-improvement? How do you work on yourself and your faults?
- Do you have a close friend who is not afraid to tell you what your faults are, when you need to be told?
- Is there someone who is close enough to you to accept your criticism?
- How do you offer your negative feedback when you think it is needed?

For Teenagers

Try to picture what Simon Peter was like. He was a very proud man, and his reputation as a fisherman was probably very important to him. It was a sad day after spending the night fishing and having nothing to show for it. But at least his reputation was somewhat protected if no one else had caught any fish either! Then along comes Jesus, and he has Simon lower the same nets from the same boat, in the same place. The result? Fish jumping all over the place! Imagine how Simon felt! Obviously, this Jesus is a miracle worker. Simon was taken aback that such a holy man would come to him—a sinner, and probably not that great a fisherman, if the truth be told. All Simon could say was, "Leave me, go away, I am a sinful man." The scene is almost comical. The great fisherman can't catch a thing all night, but this carpenter has him lower the nets once and he immediately hauls in a giant load of fish. But Jesus sticks with him: "So what if you can't catch fish? You'll be catching men and women instead."

- Have you ever been embarrassed by your sudden inability to do what you have always been able to do?
- Did you ever "freeze up" or "choke" during an athletic event, a musical performance, or a speech? What happened? How did you recover? What did your friends say? Who supported you?

We don't hear about Simon Peter's individual sins, but we know he must have been a sinner because nobody is perfect. Everyone has faults.

- What kinds of things do you think Simon Peter did that were sinful? What could have been some of his faults?
- What are some of your faults? How do you deal with them?
- What areas in your life have you improved upon?
- Do you have a close friend—so close that each of you can give the other the negative feedback that each of you needs without feeling slighted? What is that like?

For Children

Simon Peter was fishing all night, and he didn't catch any fish at all. He probably thought there weren't any fish left in the lake. Then Jesus told him to try one more time. Suddenly, the fish were jumping all over the place! Simon Peter was so surprised!

- If you were in the boat with Jesus and Simon Peter, what would you say about all the fish?
- Would you be afraid of them? Or do you think it would be fun to have fish wiggling and jumping all over you in the boat?

Peter felt sad sometimes because he wanted to be perfect for Jesus, and he wasn't perfect. He made mistakes. But Jesus helped him to feel better anyway.

- Did you ever feel sad because you couldn't do everything perfectly and you made mistakes? Who helped you to feel better?

Closing

There is so much good in the worst of us,
And so much bad in the best of us
That it hardly behooves any of us
To talk about the rest of us.
—Governor Edward Wallis Hoch (Kansas),
1849–1925

(Bartlett's Familiar Quotations)

Sixth Sunday of the Year

15 February 1998
11 February 2001
15 February 2004

Blessed Are You, Woe to You

Scripture

- *Jeremiah 17:5–8.* The person who turns away from God is cursed; but the person who trusts in God is blessed.
- *1 Corinthians 15:12,16–20.* Our faith is that Christ is risen from the dead. If our hope was limited to this life only, we would be pitiful fools.
- *Luke 6:17,20–26.* Blessed are the poor, the hungry, and the weeping; but woe to those who are rich, well-fed, and laughing.

Theme

Today is a day for looking at opposites. Sometimes we are blessed, and other times we are cursed, depending on where God is in our life. And sometimes when we are cursed by others, or by misfortune, that is when we are most blessed. How can we be blessed when we are feeling most cursed? The answer is in the paschal mystery—Jesus did not rise until after he died. Through death we receive our life. We are fools if we do not believe in a risen Christ.

How we look at comedy and tragedy can tell us a lot about our relationship with God and where we are heading.

Focusing Object

Comedy and tragedy masks, or a happy face next to a sad face

Reflections

For Adults

This Gospel makes us stop and pause. It is telling us that the times when we are hungry and poor and grieving and insulted by other people are the times when we are most blessed. Yet if we are rich and well-fed and joy-filled and praised by other people, we ought to be worried and filled with woe. What kind of message is this? It is mostly a reality check. Jesus is trying to shake us up to be sure we aren't living in a fantasy land. If we are too smug and comfortable with our luxurious situation in life, we ought to beware. Perhaps we aren't paying attention to what is really important in life, and we're drifting away from God. But if we are struggling and thirsting for truth and working for justice that doesn't seem to come, then we can take heart, for these things are bringing us closer to God.

It seems as if we don't usually stay still, as far as our relationship with God is concerned. We are either coming closer or drifting farther away. There is no such thing as neutral.

- When do you feel rich, well-fed, and joyful?
- When are you completely satisfied? Is it when you are most grateful to God and most aware of your blessings? Or is that the time when you tend to forget about God because you have no worries or fears?
- When do you feel poor and hungry and sad? Only when your own needs are not being met? Or when the needs of others are also not being met?
- When you are most desperate, is that when you cling to God and God's promise of salvation? Or is that when you curse God, lose hope, and refuse to have faith in any power beyond yourself?

This Gospel is a warning to examine the things that make us happy and sad.

- What kinds of things make you the most happy?
- If you have plenty of money, high social status, fine foods, and expensive material possessions, you might be drifting away from God. Why might this be true?
- What kinds of things make you sad?
- If you are filled with jealousy, greed, and lust, you might be drifting away from God. Why might this be true?
- If you yourself are living fairly well, yet things like poverty, oppression, and injustice still make you angry because they bring suffering to others, maybe you are coming closer to God. Why might this be true?
- If you feel joy and contentment when other people succeed, earn compliments, and experience good luck, then maybe you are coming closer to God. Why might this be true?

For Children

- When do you feel happy, like the happy face? What kinds of things happen that make you feel happy?
- When do you feel sad, like the sad face? What kinds of things happen that make you feel sad?
- When we are happy, Jesus wants us to remember people who might be sad. Why is that a good idea?
- When we are sad, Jesus wants us to remember people who might be happy. Why is that a good idea?

Closing

If we are not rising upwards
to be an angel,
depend on it, we are sinking downwards
to be a devil.
—Adapted from Samuel Taylor Coleridge
(Action 2000: C Cycle)

Seventh Sunday of the Year

22 February 1998
18 February 2001
22 February 2004

Love Everyone, Even Your Enemies

Scripture

- *1 Samuel 26:2,7–9,12–13,22–23.* Although Saul has been trying to kill David, when David has the opportunity to kill Saul, he chooses not to.
- *1 Corinthians 15:45–49.* The "first" Adam, created with Eve, was an earthly man; the "last" Adam, meaning Jesus, was a heavenly man. While on earth, we resemble Adam; once in heaven, we will resemble Jesus.
- *Luke 6:27–38.* Love your enemies, give to everyone who begs from you, and do not expect to be repaid.

Theme

We are called to resemble Jesus, who is heavenly. We are called to rise above earthly ways. The heavenly way is to love everyone, even our enemies who wish to hurt or kill us. The heavenly way is to hear the request for our coat, to give it willingly, and then to give our shirt as well.

Focusing Object
A shirt

Reflections

For Adults

- How realistic is the advice from today's Gospel? Do you think you are literally being asked to give shirts as well as coats to anyone who asks? Do you think you are literally being expected to take a slap across the face from another person and not slap back, and to give your abuser the opportunity to slap you across the face again?
- How difficult is it to live up to such standards?
- What else, besides coats and shirts, do you think Jesus is asking you to give? What is the hardest thing for you to give?

We are told to be compassionate and to pardon; to not judge and to not condemn. This way the same compassion and pardon will be shown to us, and we will be spared judgment and condemnation.

- How is your life different when you take these words seriously?
- Do you have any "enemies"?

For Teenagers

- What would you do if someone in need asked you for your coat? Would you give this person the shirt off your back as well? Why or why not? Why do you think Jesus asks you to make this sacrifice?
- What else do you think Jesus is asking you to give?
- What is the hardest thing for you to give to another person?
- When was the last time you spoke negatively of another person?
- When was the last time someone spoke negatively to you or about you?
- How would life be different if there was no judging or condemning of others—if everyone was forgiven and treated well? Why doesn't that happen?
- Do you have any "enemies"?

For Children

- Do you know anyone who wasn't nice to you?
- Jesus wants you to be nice to that person, even though he or she wasn't nice to you. Why does Jesus want you to do that? Do you think it's a good thing to do?

Jesus says that if someone needs a coat because they are cold, then we should give that person a coat, plus we should also give them a shirt.

- Do you think that would be a good thing to do?
- What other kinds of things do you think Jesus wants us to do? Why?

Closing

Consider those whom you call your enemies and figure out what they should call you. —Dwayne Dyer

(Acts of Faith)

Eighth Sunday of the Year

*25 February 2001
These readings
do not appear
in 1998 or 2004.*

Good Fruit, Good Tree

Scripture

- *Sirach 27:4–7.* You can tell what kind of tree it is by the type of fruit it bears. The same is true of people. Their words show what they are like.
- *1 Corinthians 15:54–58.* If you work hard, doing what God wants you to do, then you know that you have not worked in vain.
- *Luke 6:39–45.* The quality of the tree is shown in the fruit. Good people produce goodness. Good teachers can bring forth good students.

Theme

Jesus condemns hypocrisy more than any other sin or fault. The ones we follow need to be good people, good teachers. We don't want to be led by blind leaders. Just as we can tell trees are good by the goodness of their fruit, we can tell teachers and leaders are good by the goodness of their words and their actions.

Focusing Object
A piece of fruit

Reflections

For Adults

Just as the fruit is a reflection of the tree, it is often said that children are a reflection of their parents, or of their family.

- Have you ever worried about what others will think of you based on the actions of your children, your siblings, or your parents?
- If parents are to blame for the faults of their children, then are the parents also to be congratulated for the successes of their children?
- When is it time for the world to look at each person as an individual, responsible for her or his own faults and successes, without being a reflection of her or his parents or family?

A person of integrity acts and speaks from principles. This type of person will not say one thing and do another. This type of person is said to "walk the talk." Such a person is honest and reliable, and when a mistake is made, his or her values and motives are usually not questioned, because this person is trusted.

- Do you know many people like this? How do you know they are really trustworthy?
- Are you a person like this? How do others view you? How do you view yourself?

For Teenagers

The fruit reflects the tree, just as parents are often reflected in their sons and daughters.

- If someone said you were like your parents, would you see that as a compliment or an insult? Why?
- What do you do that makes your parents proud?
- What do you do that sometimes upsets or embarrasses your parents?
- What do your parents do that you are proud of?
- What do your parents do that you are uncomfortable with?
- Do you like being seen as a reflection of your parents, or would you prefer to be seen as an independent person, free from their influence?

Legally, if you are a minor, your parents are responsible for what you do, even if they are not at fault for your actions.

- How does that affect your decisions on how to act?

- How does that affect your parents' decisions regarding family rules?
- Do you think you are a trustworthy person?
- Do your parents trust you? Why or why not?
- Do your friends trust you? Why or why not?
- Do you trust all your friends or just some of them? Why?

For Children

- Do you think good fruit would ever grow from a bad tree? Why or why not?
- Do you think bad fruit would ever grow from a good tree? Why or why not?
- What are some ways that you are like your parents?
- What are some ways that you are not like your parents?

Closing

If you plant turnips, you will not harvest grapes.
—An Akan proverb

(Acts of Faith)

Ninth Sunday of the Year

The readings for this Sunday do not appear in Year C in 1998, 2001, or 2004.

The Centurion with Faith

Scripture

- *1 Kings 8:41–43.* Solomon prays that God will hear the prayers of foreigners who learn of God's great name and travel to Israel to pray at their Temple.
- *Galatians 1:1–2,6–10.* Paul wants people to be sure that the Gospel that is being preached is the true, authentic Gospel.
- *Luke 7:1–10.* The centurion with a sick slave asks Jesus to just speak the word so that his servant would be healed.

Theme

Authority is good to recognize. Solomon wants everyone, even foreigners, to know that the God of Israel is the one true God, and that their Temple is an authentic place to pray and to have prayers heard. Paul wants people to preach with the authority of the true Gospel. The centurion understands authority as well—he obeys the commands received from those above him, and he expects those below him to obey the commands he gives to them. He expects Jesus to have authority over all people and forces—and he has complete faith that at Jesus' word, his servant will be healed.

Focusing Object

A Red Cross first aid kit or a red cross on a white piece of paper

Reflections

For Adults

The American Red Cross is known to be the authority in disaster rescue, lifesaving techniques, and emergency supplies. People who work under their auspices and symbol are trained to follow orders and perform certain skills for saving lives. They act in a professional way, with genuine care, and they carry the credibility of their sponsor.

- Have you ever given blood? If so, did you feel as if you were in good hands?
- Have you ever taken a course in Red Cross first aid, CPR, or water safety? If so, did you feel as if you were learning valuable skills?

Jesus was known in his day as a man of power and authority in matters of forgiveness and healing. The centurion was a man who was powerful enough to have servants who submitted to his authority, yet he recognized Jesus as having power and authority greater than his own. He felt that he was not worthy to have Jesus come to his own home. He believed that Jesus had the power to heal from a distance, just by giving the order, just by saying the word.

- Who do you think is truly powerful in the world today? How so?
- Who are people that you recognize as acting with the power and authority of God?
- Who do you think is truly humble in the world today? How so?
- Is it possible to be both powerful and humble? How so?

For Teenagers

People trust the symbol of the red cross. A Red Cross first aid kit is expected to be of higher quality than any other collection of gauze, ointments, and tape. A Red Cross course in lifesaving skills is expected to meet high standards.

- Why is the symbol of the red cross so trustworthy?
- Have you ever given blood? If so, did you feel as if you were in good hands?
- Have you ever taken a course in Red Cross first aid, CPR, or water safety? If so, did you feel as if you were learning valuable skills?
- How was Jesus' reputation in this Gospel like the reputation of the Red Cross?

The centurion in the Gospel understood authority. He was powerful enough to know about giving and receiving orders, and he knew that Jesus' word was all it would take to heal his servant. Yet he was humble enough to recognize Jesus as having power and authority greater than his own.

- Have you ever felt powerful? When? What was the situation?
- Have you ever felt humble? When? What was the situation?
- Is it ever possible to be powerful and humble at the same time? How so? Do you know anyone who is? Describe that person.

For Children

- When have you seen a red cross like this? What do you think it means?
- The people from the Red Cross help people who are hurt. In today's Gospel story, how is Jesus like those people from the Red Cross?
- The centurion in the Gospel story had a lot of power. But he knew Jesus was even more powerful and could make his sick servant well again.
- If you were a centurion with a sick servant, would you have asked Jesus to come to your home to heal the servant? Or would you have asked Jesus to just say the words so that the servant would get better? Why?

Closing

Possibly the greatest risk of love is the risk of exercising power with humility.

(The Road Less Traveled)

Tenth Sunday of the Year

The readings for this Sunday do not appear in Year C in 1998, 2001, or 2004.

The Widow's Son Is Brought Back to Life

Scripture

- *1 Kings 17:17–24.* Elijah brings back to life the only son of the widow who had been showing him hospitality.
- *Galatians 1:11–19.* Paul used to persecute Christians, but he was called by Jesus to begin a new life as an Apostle.
- *Luke 7:11–17.* Jesus brings back to life the only son of a widow he meets on the street.

Theme

Jesus is like Elijah, restoring life to a widow's only son who has died. Although Paul had not experienced physical death, the change in him was also like new life. In all three stories, not only is life restored in an unexpected and miraculous way, but the faith of others is strengthened.

Focusing Object

A piece of cloth or paper, half black and half white

Reflections

For Adults

Life and death stories are very dramatic, especially when the one brought back to life is the only child of a woman without a husband and with no way to support herself. The son who was returned to life and his mother aren't the only ones to benefit from the miracle Jesus performed; reports of Jesus as a great healer, leader, and man of God spread throughout the country, causing many other people to believe in God's Chosen One.

Reports of near-death experiences and post-death experiences are fairly frequent these days, and strangely similar. A sensation of being bathed in light and feeling comfortable and peaceful is a typical report.

- Do you think these descriptions are sincere and authentic? Or do you think they are inaccurate and undependable?
- How solid is your belief in life after death? Are you completely certain, or do you have some lingering doubts about resurrection after death?
- Some of the most significant life experiences are connected with the death of a loved one or a near-death experience of our own. Why do you think this is?

For Teenagers

For most of us, death and life are like black and white. But Jesus managed to pull a young man from death right back into life. For Jesus that black and white boundary was no obstacle.

It's always a shock when someone young dies. It's easy to feel as if you are watching a person who is merely asleep when attending a young person's funeral.

- How shocking would it actually be if someone came along and helped them to arise?
- How would it change your view of death?
- Have you ever attended the funeral service for a young person—someone you were close to? Did death seem real to you at the time? What was that experience like?

For Children

Jesus and Elijah were very unusual. They each saw a very sad mother whose son had died, and they were able to make the sons come alive again. Things don't happen quite that way in our world now, because both Jesus and Elijah are in heaven.

- Is there anyone you remember who has died? What can you remember about that person?
- When someone dies, that person's family and friends come together in church to pray and to remember that person. Have you ever been to church to pray for someone who has died? What was that like?

Closing

Whoever is interested in life is particularly interested in death. —Thomas Mann

(The Promise of a New Day)

Eleventh Sunday of the Year

The readings for this Sunday do not appear in Year C in 1998, 2001, or 2004.

A Woman Anoints Jesus

Scripture

- *2 Samuel 12:7–10,13.* King David has done a terrible thing by arranging to have Uriah killed in battle so he might have Uriah's wife. Yet God forgives him.
- *Galatians 2:16,19–21.* Paul tells us that we are made right in God's eyes by our faith in Jesus Christ. Nothing we do can earn it for us.
- *Luke 7:36—8:3.* A woman known to be a sinner anoints Jesus and weeps at his feet. Simon the Pharisee finds this objectionable, but Jesus forgives her sins, and he tells Simon a parable about forgiveness.

Theme

This famous woman speaks no words and has no name. Some guess at her identity, but they are only guesses. She is sad; she weeps on Jesus' feet, wipes them with her hair, and anoints them with ointment from an alabaster jar. She is known to be a sinner, but Jesus makes her actions his classic example of hospitality and care. He forgives her all her sins and tells her to go in peace because her faith has saved her.

Focusing Object
A bottle of skin lotion

Reflections

For Adults

This woman with no name speaks volumes with no words. She is branded as a sinner, yet Jesus calls all of us to follow her example.

- When have you witnessed someone speaking volumes without saying a word? When have someone's actions been that powerful?

Jesus reminds us that forgiving debts is like forgiving wrongs. The greater the sin, the greater the gift of forgiveness.

- Think of the greatest hurt anyone has caused you. Have you forgiven that hurt, or are you still nursing it? How long ago did this situation occur? How did this affect your life? Does it still have an influence in your life? How so?

For Teenagers

This is a mysterious woman. She didn't say anything, and we don't really know for sure what her name was or what her sin was. She entered into someone else's house, shed tears all over Jesus' feet, wiped them with her own hair, and then rubbed ointment, which is like lotion, all over them. The person whose house Jesus was visiting was not happy that she came in, uninvited, and made such a spectacle of herself. Yet Jesus seemed peaceful and comfortable with the situation. He was actually quite touched.

- How would you respond if you were visiting someone and a girl you didn't know came in the door and did this to you? What would you say? What would you do?
- What if a girl came to your house and did these things to one of your friends? Would you feel responsible? What would your reaction be?

Jesus used the actions of this woman as an example for others to follow. But what she did isn't exactly customary in this century, with our different social expectations.

- If Jesus came today and the same situation took place, with a modern updating, what kind of gesture might be comparable to the washing and anointing of Jesus' feet?

For Children

We don't really know this woman's name, and she doesn't say anything to anybody. But we know she cares about Jesus, and Jesus says that is what's important.

- Do you know someone who cares about you? What kinds of things does that person do without talking to show you that she or he cares about you?
- If you wanted to do something special for someone, without talking, what would you do?

Closing

Well done is better than well said. —Benjamin Franklin

Twelfth Sunday of the Year

21 June 1998
24 June 2001
20 June 2004

Who Do You Say That I Am?

Scripture

- *Zechariah 12:10–11*. The house of David and the citizens of Jerusalem will be filled with compassion, so they will mourn the one they have pierced.
- *Galatians 3:26–29*. Our unity comes from Jesus. There is no reason to be labeled as Jew or Greek, male or female, slave or free.
- *Luke 9:18–24*. Jesus asks his followers, "Who do you say that I am?" and Peter answers, "The Christ." Jesus tells them that he will be rejected and killed.

Theme

Who am I? This is an important question that everyone asks. We are the descendants of Abraham and Sarah, united with Jesus. We are descendants of the inhabitants of Jerusalem, who have come to know the significance of the death of Jesus. We are followers of the Christ, God's Anointed One, and we know that means that we have to take up our cross daily in order to follow.

Focusing Object
An ID card

Reflections

For Adults

When Jesus asked his followers who the people thought he might be, different answers were given: Elijah, John the Baptist, one of the older prophets. Only those closest to Jesus knew who he really was—the Messiah.

- What is your general reputation? If someone who has heard of you (but doesn't know you well) was asked about you, what response would you guess might be given?
- How well do your closest friends know you? What would they say about who you really are?

We get lots of strong messages about who we need to be, and a lot of pressure to fulfill someone else's idea of who we should be. The pressure can come from our employer, our spouse, our family, our friends, and even the media. To discover who we really are takes quite a search for the truth.

- What are some of the messages you hear that pressure you to become a certain kind of person? Which are helpful? Which are not?
- Jesus expects us to take up our cross daily. What do you think that means for you?

For Teenagers

Reputation is very significant—in school, in the workplace, and in the community. A person who is thought to be responsible and honest is treated with respect. A person who is thought to be untrustworthy is treated with suspicion. Sometimes the way we dress or the way we speak affects our reputation.

- Who do people say you are—especially people who aren't your closest friends and don't know you very well?
- Who would your closest friends say you are?
- Who would your family say you are?
- How are any of the above answers different from what you would say about who you are?

- What is the real truth that you have come to know about who you are? Do you know yourself completely, or is the search for that truth still continuing?

There was confusion about who Jesus was. He had quite a colorful reputation. Only his closest followers knew that he was the Messiah.

- Who is Jesus to you now? Since he no longer walks the earth in his own flesh and blood, how can you have a relationship with him?
- How does he affect your life?

For Children

Some people were mixed up about who Jesus was. But Jesus' friends knew that he was the savior sent by God.

- If someone asked you what you knew about Jesus, what would you tell them?
- If someone asked one of your friends about who you were, what do you think your friend would say about you?

Closing

You must do your own independent investigation of truth. —A Bahá'í teaching

(Acts of Faith)

Thirteenth Sunday of the Year

28 June 1998
1 July 2001
27 June 2004

Nowhere to Lay My Head

Scripture

- *1 Kings 19:16,19–21.* Elisha is willing to give up his whole life to follow Elijah and be his successor.
- *Galatians 5:1,13–18.* Christ set us free—but free to be people of love and service, guided by the Spirit.
- *Luke 9:51–62.* Jesus is teaching us what it takes to be a disciple. We must be willing to give up our whole life in order to serve.

Theme

Elisha slaughters his animals and destroys his farming equipment before following Elijah. His whole previous life is over. Paul teaches us that we are freed by Jesus to follow the Spirit, in love and service to each other, being careful not to bite and tear each other up in the process. Jesus stresses the cost of discipleship—giving up your whole life to follow, and not always having a place to lay your head.

Focusing Object
A pillow

Reflections

For Adults

Foxes and birds can retreat to their lairs and nests, but Jesus was homeless. On his way to Jerusalem he was not welcomed in the Samaritan town where he stopped, so he had to continue to the next town, looking for a place to rest.

The cost of discipleship is high—sometimes you have nowhere to go, but you just keep following where the Spirit leads you, even when you don't understand where that will take you. Parenting can be like that. So can working on a career that is demanding and stressful for short spurts of time.

- Why do people continue the effort to achieve their goals in life? What drives them? Where do they get the energy?
- Is there a goal in your life that saps your energy, demands all your attention, and becomes the focus of your life—at least for a while? What is your motive for trying to achieve this goal?

People are not able to perform, work, and expend energy without rest and replenishment. The result from that stress is usually some kind of sickness—your body will tell you when you've crossed the line.

- What do you do in your life to manage that stress? How do you take care of yourself—physically and mentally?

For Teenagers

Jesus is telling us how hard it is to be a follower. Sometimes we have to make sacrifices and give up part of our life. Sometimes we will have no place to rest our head because our schedule is so intense or because we are not among friends.

- What do you think it means to be a follower of Jesus? What hardships might it entail?
- Is anything worth these hardships? Who could dedicate their life to anything so demanding?
- Do you think Jesus was exaggerating to make a point?

- Religious life, marriage, parenting, and certain careers make incredible demands on one's life. What do you think are the most demanding life choices? How so?
- What would you be willing to make life-sacrifices for? What sacrifices would you make?

For Children

Jesus was tired, but he had no place to sleep. Nobody in that town wanted him to stay there, so he had to keep walking to find the next town.

- When it gets late, do you go right to bed or do you fight your parents to stay up later, even though you are tired?
- Did you ever walk a long, long time? Where did you go? How tired did you get from walking? Did you ever want to stop and yet had no place to rest? What was that like?
- If you lived in that town, what would you say to the people who didn't want Jesus to stay overnight with them? Would you invite Jesus to stay at your house? Why or why not?

Closing

Saints must sleep and even prophets must play.

(The Road Less Traveled)

Fourteenth Sunday of the Year

5 July 1998
8 July 2001
4 July 2004

Sending Workers for the Harvest

Scripture

- *Isaiah 66:10–14.* Rejoice and return to Jerusalem, a symbol of the house of God, where you will be welcomed as a mother welcomes and comforts her children.
- *Galatians 6:14–18.* Paul is defending his status as an Apostle—the scars from his floggings and stonings mark him as a follower of Jesus.
- *Luke 10:1–12,17–20.* The harvest is rich but the laborers are few. So Jesus sends seventy-two disciples, in pairs, to visit towns, cure the sick, and preach. They return successful and rejoicing.

Theme

The harvest master needs workers for the harvest. There are so few workers that the task seems impossible. But Jesus sends out the seventy-two disciples, in pairs, with confidence. They return in jubilation, welcomed by Jesus with open arms, the way Isaiah describes the welcoming and return to Jerusalem. They seem to do the impossible. But like Paul, they are clearly marked as followers of Jesus, and perhaps, like Paul, they have a few scars to show for it.

Focusing Object

A gardening tool or the number 72

Reflections

What impossible work—to be sent out as lambs among wolves, but to go with confidence, knowing you are sent by Jesus.

• Have you ever begun such an impossible task—not knowing how things would turn out, but knowing it was the right thing to do? Did you have any support? Or did people assume you would fail? What happened?

Thirty-six pairs of people walked to different towns, without any luggage, without much of a plan, not knowing where they would be staying or how they would be received. Yet they journeyed.

• When you travel, what is the biggest stress? What is the worst inconvenience of not being at home?

• Would you ever travel to a foreign land under the conditions described in the Gospel?

• Do you enjoy travel enough to see such a situation as an adventure? Or is traveling, even to a familiar place, so stressful that you would never want to go someplace without a planned itinerary?

• What meaning does the story of the sending of the seventy-two have for your life journey?

We don't know their names, but we know that three dozen pairs—thirty-six partnerships—set out on this adventure, not knowing what to expect. They took no suitcases, no supplies, no map, and they had no plan. Yet they trusted Jesus, and they went because the harvest was ready and there weren't many workers. Jesus needed them.

• Would you have gone on such a journey if you had been around in those days with Jesus and he asked you to? Why or why not?

• If you wanted to go on a mission trip with a church group that had the same expectations as this trip with the seventy-two—no luggage, no plan, no supplies, and the like—would your parents let you go? Why or why not?

- Would you be willing to do it as an adult? Why or why not?
- Do Jesus' instructions for the seventy-two disciples have any meaning for your life journey?

These seventy-two followers seemed to "do the impossible." They had a mission, they had confidence, and they succeeded.

- Have you ever attempted to do the impossible? What happened? Were you successful? What did others think?

For Children

Jesus sent out some of his friends to cure people who were sick, and to teach everyone about God. They had never done any teaching before, and they hadn't ever cured anyone who was sick, either.

- Do you think they were afraid to go? Would you be afraid to go?
- Do you ever talk to anyone about Jesus? Who do you talk to? What do you say?
- Have you ever helped to take care of someone who was sick? What did you do? Did the person get better?

Closing

The bumblebee's wings are so thin and its body so big, it should not be able to fly. The only problem is, the bee doesn't know that. —David Lindsey

(Acts of Faith)

Fifteenth Sunday of the Year

12 July 1998
15 July 2001
11 July 2004

The Good Samaritan

Scripture

- *Deuteronomy 30:10–14.* The command that Moses is telling his people about is "Choose life." It is already in our mouth and heart.
- *Colossians 1:15–20.* Jesus is the image of the invisible God who is above all things, all angels, all creation, everything.
- *Luke 10:25–37.* Jesus tells the story of the good Samaritan, the outcast, who was the only one to show compassion to a stranger in need.

Theme

The most important law is not far away or difficult to understand. It is already in our heart, because it is the law of love. Jesus lived the law of love and shows us how to do the same. Jesus chooses a Samaritan to be the hero of his story, knowing that Jews are taught to despise Samaritans. Telling us this story about love is an excellent example of his own love.

Focusing Object
An Ace bandage

Reflections

For Adults

In the previous chapter of Luke's Gospel, Jesus is rejected by the people in a Samaritan town. Yet, he still uses a Samaritan in his story to teach us how we should act.

- Have you ever been rejected or treated badly? Would you be likely to later speak highly of that person, or of the people related to that person?
- Does your treatment by one person affect your perception of related people? Why or why not?

Jesus tells us this story to illustrate the need for us to get involved in the suffering of others.

- When have you taken action to get involved in addressing others who are suffering or in need?
- When have you chosen to not get involved in other's problems? What was usually your reason? Were you too busy? Were you afraid for your own safety? Did you feel uncomfortable? Did you think that you did not have enough money to help? Did you doubt the urgency or seriousness of the situation?
- What are other reasons that people choose to not get involved?

For Teenagers

Samaritans had a bad reputation among Jews. Jews regarded them as bad examples, people to avoid, people who did not follow God's law. Yet Jesus made a Samaritan the hero in his story. The priest and the Levite are people Jews were taught to respect and imitate, and yet Jesus made them the selfish and uncaring people in his story.

- Besides telling us to get involved and help other people, what else do you think Jesus was trying to teach us with this story?
- If Jesus came to us today, in our modern culture, how would he tell this story to get the same point across?

Sometimes we avoid getting involved with strangers because it might be dangerous, and sometimes we avoid it because we might have to spend some time and energy, or because we would feel awkward in doing so.

- What is an example of a dangerous situation when most people would agree that it would not be a good idea to get involved with a stranger in need?
- What is an example of a situation when it would not be dangerous for you to get involved with a stranger in need?
- What is an example of a situation involving a stranger in need that is difficult to decide upon— a situation that isn't completely dangerous, but isn't completely safe either? What would you do in that situation? What advice would you give regarding appropriate action to take in that situation?

For Children

Lots of Jesus' friends didn't like the Samaritan people because they didn't pray to God the way Jesus' friends did. In the story of the good Samaritan, Jesus is teaching that what really counts with God is caring for people who are in need.

- Have you ever stayed away from some people your age because others didn't like them?
- Have you ever done something good for a person that everyone else put down or made fun of? How did that feel? What happened that time?

Most of us try to be as nice to others as we can, but sometimes we join in hurting others.

- Did you ever hurt someone because everyone else was doing so? Did you ever tell someone you hurt that you were sorry? What happened?

Closing

The most frightening part of helping is getting involved. —Diane Ridley Roberts

(Acts of Faith)

Sixteenth Sunday of the Year

19 July 1998
22 July 2001
18 July 2004

Martha and Mary

Scripture

- *Genesis 18:1–10.* God appeared to Abraham as three visitors, and Abraham showed them fine hospitality. Abraham was told that his wife, Sarah, would give birth to a son.
- *Colossians 1:24–28.* Paul speaks of his joy (despite his suffering) of being a minister to the church.
- *Luke 10:38–42.* Jesus visits Martha and Mary. Martha is tending to the household needs of hospitality while Mary sits and listens to Jesus.

Theme

Hospitality is very important. Abraham is hospitable to three strangers, and then receives the marvelous news that he will have a son with his wife, Sarah. Jesus visits Martha and Mary and, in their different ways, they both attend to the needs of hospitality. Good and effective ministry, which Paul speaks of, involves the element of hospitality.

Focusing Object

A kettle, a teapot, or a coffeepot

Reflections

Mary and Martha are both attending to hospitality. Martha runs around preparing food and getting cups and bowls ready. Mary puts all her energy into listening to what Jesus has to say. Martha is anxious about making things perfect for Jesus, but Jesus tells her that what Mary has chosen to do at that time is very important.

- Have you ever hosted a large party for friends or family? Have you ever found yourself so busy with the tasks of cooking, serving, and other preparations that you hardly had any time at all to talk to your guests?
- What is that feeling like? Does that feel like a successful party, or do you feel like the whole event was ruined by your busyness and level of activity?
- Do you think Jesus is trying to tell us that keeping our house clean and having food available to offer to guests is not important? What do you think is his main message?
- When you go to someone's home to visit, what is more important to you: that the placemats and napkins match the flowers in the centerpiece, or that the person you are visiting is paying attention to you, listening to you, and enjoying your company?

For Teenagers

Martha and Mary are often seen as symbols for a balance of hospitality. Martha represents the tasks of preparation—cleaning house, cooking food, setting out the dishes and cups, and the like. Mary represents the personal care of the visitor—listening, paying attention, spending quality time in conversation. Both are important.

- If you were invited to someone's home for dinner and the house was a total mess and no food was prepared, but the person cleared the junk off the sofa so you both would have a place to sit and visit, how would you feel?

- If you were invited to someone's home for dinner and the gourmet meal was so complicated that you were completely ignored until dinner was on the table, how would you feel?

Some people are the "perfect blend" of the Martha-Mary examples of hospitality, but others fall off to one side or the other, being more talkers than housekeepers, or being more housekeepers than talkers.

- When you have people over, do you tend to be more of a talker or more of a housekeeper? Or do you think you have a good balance, having all the preparations done ahead of time so that the focus for your attention is your guest?
- Do you know anyone who has a perfect balance?

For Children

Martha and Mary were friends of Jesus. When Jesus came over, both of his friends wanted to be sure Jesus had a good time.

- Martha wanted to be sure that the table was set and that there was good food to eat. Why is that important to do if you are having company over for dinner?
- Mary wanted to be sure that Jesus was enjoying himself and not feeling lonely or bored. Why is that important to do if you are having company over for dinner?

Closing

By far, the most important form of attention we can give our loved ones is listening.

(Adapted from *The Road Less Traveled*)

Seventeenth Sunday of the Year

26 July 1998
29 July 2001
25 July 2004

Ask and You Will Receive

Scripture

- *Genesis 18:20–32.* Abraham asks Yahweh for mercy for the sake of the innocent and receives it.
- *Colossians 2:12–14.* Because of our faith we have new life, and all our sins are pardoned.
- *Luke 11:1–13.* Jesus teaches us to pray and assures us that our prayers will be answered if we ask, seek, and knock.

Theme

Faith in prayer is stressed in these readings. Abraham is persistent, and he manages to persuade Yahweh to not destroy the cities for the sake of even ten innocent people. Paul tells us that our faith is what will raise us to new life. Jesus is observed praying and, in response to his disciples' request, teaches them how to pray, emphasizing persistence.

Focusing Object
A copy of the Lord's Prayer

Reflections

For Adults

Jesus uses loving parents and their responses to their children as an image to understand the relationship between God and us. We would not give our children snakes and scorpions if they needed fish or eggs. So, too, God will give us what we need.

- If you are a parent, what do your children ask you for? Do they always need the things they ask for? What is your response if they ask for things they don't need (or should not have)?
- If you are not a parent, what do you imagine you would do in that situation if you were a parent?

Jesus teaches us to pray: "Subject us not to the trial." We pray to not be led to temptation, but often we have a choice. Sometimes we lead ourselves to temptation, knowing full well what we are doing.

- What are your temptations? How do you stay away from them?

For Teenagers

Jesus teaches us to ask, to seek, and to knock. If we do, we are promised that we shall receive, we shall find, and doors will be opened for us.

- Does this mean that prayers are a type of magic and that all we have to do is pray and we can control the outcome of the world? If not, what do you think it means?

Jesus teaches us to pray: "Forgive us our sins, for we too forgive all who do us wrong."

- Is there anyone who has done you wrong whom you cannot forgive? What gets in the way of your forgiveness?
- If all our sins are forgiven anyway, why should we even try to resist temptation? Why not just continue to sin if we can always be forgiven? What would Jesus say to that proposition?

For Children

Jesus taught us to pray the prayer that we now call the "Lord's Prayer," or the "Our Father."

- Do you know this prayer by heart? If so, can you say it with me now?
- What do you think that prayer means? What are some of the words that you understand?
- What are some of the words that you don't understand?

- If Jesus was here now, and you could ask him, "How do you want us to pray?" what do you think he would tell you?

Closing

I can resist anything but temptation. —Oscar Wilde

(Success Every Day)

Eighteenth Sunday of the Year

2 August 1998
5 August 2001
1 August 2004

Piling Up Possessions

Scripture

- *Ecclesiastes 1:2; 2:21–23.* Qoheleth says that without God, life is vanity! All things are useless! What's the point? There's just no use.
- *Colossians 3:1–5,9–11.* Paul warns us to pay attention to what is most important, not to earthly desires that get us nowhere.
- *Luke 12:13–21.* Jesus teaches us that it is a waste to be greedy and to pile up possessions. They will not get us any closer to God.

Theme

Don't be greedy! All the wealth in the world won't get us to heaven! If we are to put our energy into anything, let it not be useless earthly desires that only lead to boredom and dissatisfaction. Material things are useless in themselves—there's no point to living if we don't live for God.

Focusing Object
A picture of a barn

Reflections

For Adults

The rich man with an abundant harvest made a decision. His barn was not big enough to hold all his grain. So he pulled down his barn and built a bigger one to hold all his grain and possessions. Jesus said he died that night, a rich fool.

There is reason to plan ahead and to be able to provide for the future. But that can get out of hand and lead to greed.

- What is the balance between being greedy and providing for the future?
- How do you decide what amount of money to save for yourself or your family and what amount to give to the church and other charities?
- How do you decide how much time to spend at work, to spend with your friends or your family, and to spend in service to others in need?

The media constantly bombard us with consumer materialism images that teach us to see ourselves in need of countless products that we don't actually need. Buying them usually makes others rich, but leaves us greedy, dissatisfied with ourselves, and wondering what is wrong.

- How do you keep from becoming too materialistic? When you see ads for things you don't need but would not mind having, are you easily convinced to buy them, or are you a "hard sell"?

For Teenagers

Money can make life a little easier to manage at times, but a famous proverb proclaims that "money can't buy happiness."

- Do you think most people believe that proverb?
- Why are so many people so easily convinced that having more of this or that will make their life better?
- What types of ads are you most susceptible to? What do you end up buying or wanting to buy most often?
- Are you an impulse buyer? Or do you not spend money unless you have planned to spend it on something you truly need?

Jesus tells us about the man who tore down his grain bins to build bigger ones in order to contain all his grain. Jesus called this man a fool.

- Do you have room in your closets for all your clothes and possessions?
- When your closets get too full, are you more likely to find more storage space in your house, or are you more likely to go through your things and decide what you use and don't use?
- Once you have some extra clothing or other items that you no longer want to keep, what do you do? Do you throw them away? Do you give them to agencies such as Goodwill Industries and the Salvation Army? Do you sell them at a yard sale to make more money?

For Children

Jesus tells us this story about a man who had so much food that it wouldn't fit in his barn. Instead of giving it away to other people who needed the food, this man decided to tear down his barn and build a bigger barn so he could keep all his extra food for himself. Jesus said this person was greedy. He didn't want to share.

- What do you think Jesus would have wanted this greedy man to do? What advice would you give to the man with all the food?
- Can you think of a time that you shared something of yours? What was it? Who did you share it with?

Closing

Possession of material riches without inner peace is like dying of thirst while bathing in the river.
—Paramhansa Yogananda

(Acts of Faith)

Nineteenth Sunday of the Year

9 August 1998
12 August 2001
8 August 2004

Be Ready at All Times

Scripture

- *Wisdom 18:6–9.* On "that night," the Passover, the people knew ahead of time what was to happen. Because of their faith, they had courage and did what they needed to do.
- *Hebrews 11:1–2,8–19.* Because of our faith, we can be sure about things that are uncertain; we can know how we need to act. Abraham and Sarah are given as examples of people acting from faith.
- *Luke 12:32–48.* We are warned by Jesus to be prepared and to do our work well. If we have heavenly treasure, no thief can come near it. If we stay alert, then we are ready, whether it is the thief or the master who comes.

Theme

We need faith in God—but faith alone is not enough. We also must be ready to do the things our faith calls us to do. Moses, with faith, led the Israelites to perform the rituals of the Passover, to leave Egypt, and so to be freed from their slavery. Abraham and Sarah had faith and did what God asked—they moved to a new place, had a son in their old age, and were even willing to sacrifice that son. Jesus calls us to do likewise. We have been given a lot, and a lot is expected of us.

Focusing Object

A key

Reflections

For Adults

A servant who is trusted is given the key to the master's house. Much is expected of that servant. The master expects the house in order at all times. No matter the time of the return, the house will be in proper order, and the master will approve of the work that has been done.

- If you are the servant and God is the master, what tasks do you think God wants you to do in the household? What is the "thief" you need to be alert to?

We need faith, but we also need to act—to make things happen. Our faith, our prayer life, and our relationship to God make sure that the things we are working toward are the things of heavenly treasure, and not just things that moths can destroy or thieves can steal.

- What are your earthly treasures? How devastated would you be if they were ruined by moths, thieves, fire, floods, tornadoes, earthquakes, hurricanes, or whatever else could happen?
- What are your heavenly treasures? How much of your time and energy gets focused on them?

For Teenagers

The key to the house is a symbol of trust and responsibility.

- Do you have your own house key? If so, how often do you use it?
- Are there any house rules about the key or about what is to happen when you are home alone?
- If you don't have your own key, would you like to have one? Do you need one? Why or why not?

This talk of servants being ready for masters and thieves to catch them off their guard can be easily translated to teenagers being ready for parents and teachers to catch them off their guard.

- If you could stay home for a week with no parental supervision, what would you do in the house?
- If your parents suddenly returned home several days early, do you think they would be pleased with the state of your house, or angry with the way they found things?
- If your teachers decided to give you no tests and no homework until the end of each term, would you keep up with your studies on your own? Why or why not? What do you think the rest of your friends would do?
- What do you think it means to have God return to your house expecting things to be in proper order?

For Children

Having a key to the house means you can lock the door and unlock the door when no one else is home. It means you are trusted. Jesus wants us to be trustworthy.

- Do you have a key to your house? If you do, how old were you when you got the key? Do you like having your own key? Do you come home by yourself a lot, or only once in a while?
- If you don't have a key to your house, how old do you think you will be when you get one? Do you want one? Why or why not?
- Does the idea of staying home alone for a long time sound scary, or does it sound exciting? What would you do if you were home by yourself?

Closing

Work as though all depends on you.
Pray as though all depends on God.
　　　　　　　—Saint Ignatius of Loyola
　　　　　　　　　　(Vision 2000: A Cycle)

Twentieth Sunday of the Year

16 August 1998
19 August 2001
The readings
for this Sunday do
not occur in 2004.

Jeremiah in the Well

Scripture

○ *Jeremiah 38:4–6,8–10.* Jeremiah is thrown into a well when he preaches an unpopular message. Although some believe his message, most do not.

● *Hebrews 12:1–4.* It is a struggle to be a follower of Jesus. But we are encouraged to keep running the race that lies ahead of us, and to keep our eyes fixed on Jesus.

● *Luke 12:49–53.* Jesus warns that even households will be divided over who will believe in him. In the same house, some will believe and some will not.

Theme

Jeremiah is rejected by some who throw him into a well, but rescued by others who receive him. Jesus foresees the same thing happening to him, warning that what he stands for will even divide households—sons against fathers, mothers against daughters. Running with Christ is not an easy race to run, but if we keep our focus on our faith, we can finish the race despite the opposition we are sure to face.

Focusing Object

A small container of mud or a picture of a well

Reflections

Jerusalem is facing a major battle, a battle they cannot win. If they surrender to the Babylonians, they will at least survive and not be killed. Jeremiah advises surrender, but no one wants to hear it. Instead of seeing him as a great prophet, he is seen as a threat to the confidence and morale of soldiers and citizens. He is thrown into a well as punishment.

- Have you ever been "punished" for speaking the truth that no one else wanted to hear? What happened?
- Who are some other people—famous or not—who have attempted to speak the truth, only to be punished by severe consequences such as loss of job, loss of reputation, or even death?

Throughout this whole reading, Jeremiah does not speak. We don't know if he is shaking his fist in anger, crying in fear, or if he is on his knees praying for a rescue from all that mud at the bottom of the well.

- Use your imagination. If you were in Jeremiah's situation, what would you be saying or thinking or doing?
- How do you usually respond when you are put in an uncomfortable or even dangerous situation because of someone else's actions?

Jeremiah is stuck in the mud at the bottom of a well. He was thrown in there because he said that God wanted Jerusalem to surrender to Babylon in order to save their own lives—a message the people did not want to hear. He was a prophet who was being punished for speaking the truth. People don't like to hear what they don't want to do—they would rather blame the speaker and pretend the message is wrong than listen to the truth.

Modern-day prophets likewise try to warn people about what will happen if we don't change. Books, movies, and television specials try to warn us about things like population growth, pollution levels, un healthy ingredients in foods, the waste of natural resources, the ruin of rain forests, corruption in government or industry, and so forth.

- Which modern-day prophets do you listen to? Which ones do you want to ignore? Why?

Although Jeremiah is stuck at the bottom of the muddy well, he is not completely abandoned. He has a few loyal supporters to help him get out. The Scripture verses that follow the readings for this Sunday explain how Ebed-melech got some rags from the palace linen closet and lowered them into the well with the ropes. He told Jeremiah to put the rags under his armpits so the ropes would not cut and burn them. Ebed-melech was obviously kind and courageous.

- Do you have such a loyal friend who might help you out if you were unjustly punished? Has such a thing ever happened to you? What was the outcome?
- We never hear a word about Jeremiah's words or feelings or thoughts. He is silent throughout this whole ordeal. What do you think he felt or thought or said? What do you think he did in that well? Do you think he prayed or cried or screamed out loud? What would you do?

For Children

Jeremiah was a good and truthful man, but people didn't want to hear what he had to say. So the king let them do a nasty thing—they put Jeremiah down into a muddy well.

- Did you ever get in trouble after telling the truth? If so, what happened?
- Have you ever seen a well? If so, what did it look like? Were you able to get water from it?
- If you have never seen a real well, have you seen one in a book or a movie? Who uses wells?

Wells are used to get water from the ground. But sometimes the water runs out, and nothing is left at the bottom but mud. That's the kind of well Jeremiah was stuck in.

- What do you think it was like for Jeremiah? Do you think the mud was warm or cold down in the well? Do you think he felt dirty or clean there?
- If you were there when they put Jeremiah in the well, what would you have done?
- If Jeremiah wanted to talk to you while he waited for the people to rescue him, what would you say to him?

Closing

Certain thoughts are prayers.
There are moments when,
whatever the attitude of the body,
the soul is on its knees.
—Victor Hugo
(Action 2000: C Cycle)

Twenty-First Sunday of the Year

23 August 1998
26 August 2001
22 August 2004

Discipline

Scripture

- *Isaiah 66:18–21.* People from all nations will come and proclaim God's glory. These foreigners will be welcomed and honored—some even as priests.
- *Hebrews 12:5–7,11–13.* God disciplines us with the same love and concern that mothers or fathers use to discipline their children. We need discipline to grow and be strong.
- *Luke 13:22–30.* People from the north, south, east, and west will come and want a place at the feast of God. Yet some of those last shall enter first, and some of those first shall be last.

Theme

Isaiah tells us that people from every foreign land will be brought to Jerusalem by every means possible—camels, mules, carts, chariots, and the like. Some of these foreigners will be given the honor of priesthood. This is a surprise to Jews who are taught to avoid Gentiles. Jesus has a similar surprise for us—some people assumed to be rejected will be accepted, and some people expecting to be accepted will be rejected.

How can we improve our chances of admission through this narrow door? By heeding the gentle discipline that God gives us.

Focusing Object

A list of classroom rules, family chores, or parish policies

Reflections

For Adults

No one escapes pain and suffering; it comes with being mortal creatures. Yet, God brings good out of it by turning it into an opportunity for strengthening and disciplining us. Pain and suffering can be seen as the discipline of God.

- Is this clear in your life? Do you believe it to be true? Can suffering actually make you a better person? How has this been true in your life?
- How do you respond to suffering and problems? Has this response changed over the years? How are you different from when you were younger?

Discipline from God is different than discipline from the church, the government, your employer, or even your family.

- How do you respond to the enforcement of laws and policies that come from the church? from the government? from your employer? from your own parents or older relatives?
- Which of these sources of discipline are hardest to deal with? Which are the easiest? Why?
- If you have children, or if your work involves teaching or supervising children or young people, what kind of disciplinarian are you?
- What are the challenges of disciplining the young?

For Teenagers

Life's problems can be seen as challenges that help you to grow well and to learn important skills. As God's creatures are imperfect, so we need to help one another toward a final perfection that is a gift from God.

- What difficulty or crisis in your life has taught you a lot? Do you think you have grown from dealing with it? How?

Discipline from parents and teachers and coaches is often not desired, yet it is usually given because of love.

- What do you think motivates parents and teachers and coaches? Why do they do the things they do for you? What is their purpose as they attempt to give you discipline?
- How have you benefited from the discipline and influence of parents, teachers, or coaches? Have other adults in your life helped you become a more mature individual? Who are they and what influence have they had?

For Children

God loves us. Our parents and teachers love us, too. That's why they give us rules. Rules help make life go smoother.
- What are some rules that make your house a better place to live in?
- What are some rules that make school a better place to learn in?
- If you were in charge of your house or your school, what rules would you make? Which rules would you get rid of?

Closing

Things turn out best for those who make the best of the way things turn out. —Art Linkletter

Twenty-Second Sunday of the Year

30 August 1998
2 September 2001
29 August 2004

Choose a Humble Seat

Scripture

- *Sirach 3:17–18,20,28–29.* Be humble. The more important a person you perceive yourself to be, the greater the need to be humble.
- *Hebrews 12:18–19,22–24.* Coming to God is not like a trip with Moses to a tall, dark, gloomy mountain to get the tablets of the Law. No, it is like a warm, loving gathering where you are greeted by angels and brought to a heavenly feast.
- *Luke 14:1,7–14.* When you come to a feast, do not choose a place of high honor to sit. A more important person may need your seat. Instead, sit at a lower position, so you might be asked to come to a better seat.

Theme

Humility is joy. Those who are humble are treated well by others. They bring joy, and they receive joy in return. This is true when we approach a wedding feast or when we approach the heavenly feast of God's banquet.

Focusing Object

A placemat or place setting, or a table and chairs (doll-furniture size)

Reflections

For Adults

Jesus advises us to not sit at the head of the table, but to choose a place of lower status.

- What is the status of your position at work, in your community, or even in your family?
- Does your status have any privileges that are not given to others? If so, what are they?
- How do others feel about not sharing in the privileges you are given?
- If your status is lower than most, are there any privileges that others have and you do not? What are they? How do you feel about that?

Jesus challenges us to include persons with disabilities in our social activities.

- Do you have any friends who are blind or deaf, who use a wheelchair, or who have another disability? If so, how did you meet?
- Do you think it is appropriate to go out of your way to make friends with people with disabilities? Why or why not?

For Teenagers

Jesus advises us to be humble, and not to assume that we have a higher position or status than others. That way we won't be embarrassed if someone else comes along whose status is actually higher than ours.

A lot of status-lowering is done with put-downs. Every time you put someone down, it is an attempt to lower that person's status and to raise your own.

- How does status-lowering relate to what Jesus asks us to do?
- Paying a compliment to another person raises their status. If your compliment is accepted with grace, your status is also raised. If your compliment is rejected, or coupled with a put-down against you, your status is then lowered. How often does this happen?
- It seems to be more of a risk to compliment a person than it is to put someone down. Yet Jesus asks us to take that risk. Are you willing to risk giving compliments?

- Are you willing to stop dishing out put-downs and to start giving more compliments to others? Why or why not? What would Jesus say about this decision?

Jesus challenges us to include people of the lowest status in our social activities.

- When you have a party or when you are in the position of inviting someone to go to a movie or an athletic event with you, do you tend to seek out the most popular people with the highest social status? Or do you seek out the people who are least popular and sometimes made fun of? Why?
- Do you think Jesus' challenge is unrealistic, or do you think it is what the world needs? How so?
- What would Jesus tell teenagers directly if he were a verbal, flesh-and-blood part of this conversation?

For Children

Jesus tells us to be careful where we sit when we go to a party. He says we should treat everyone else as if they are very important, because they are. And we shouldn't sit down in an important place, because that place might belong to someone else.

- Have you ever been to a fancy party or a fancy restaurant? What was it like? Where did you sit? Did someone help you to know where to sit? What kind of food did you eat there? What was the best part about going there?
- At your home, when you sit down to eat supper together, where does everyone sit? Do you sit in the same place all the time or does your place change?
- Do you like where you sit at the supper table? Why or why not?

Closing

Get someone else to blow your horn and the sound will carry twice as far. —Will Rogers

(Go for the Gold)

Twenty-Third Sunday of the Year

6 September 1998
9 September 2001
5 September 2004

First Calculate, Then Build

Scripture

- *Wisdom 9:13–18.* King Solomon muses about how little we can understand when it comes to God's intentions and plans. Any glimpse we get of understanding comes from the Holy Spirit.
- *Philemon 1:9–10,12–17.* From behind bars, Paul writes to Philemon about Onesimus, a slave of Philemon, whom he met in prison. Paul urges Philemon to accept Onesimus back as a brother, and to free him from slavery so he can become one of Paul's coworkers.
- *Luke 14:25–33.* Jesus reminds us of all the planning and work we put into building a tower or waging a battle. At least that much sacrifice and effort must go into being one of his followers.

Theme

The universe God has created is so immense and complicated that we could never hope to understand it, even though we act as if we do so in our plans for towers, wars, industrial and business operations, and other complicated projects. We invest a lot of energy in these earthly projects. Sometimes they are the focus of our entire life. Jesus is asking us to invest that much energy into being a dedicated follower.

Focusing Object
Building blocks, three or four in a stack

Jesus requests that anyone who wishes to follow him abandon everything, including family, so that all energy can go into being a disciple. This sounds a little harsh until we realize how some of us give up our whole life and even our family for other pursuits. Star athletes, musicians, and dancers often begin dedicating their entire life to their talent and craft when they are children. Many go to special schools, away from home, and literally give up their childhood in order to succeed.

- When you hear of dedication such as this, are you inspired by it, or are you angry with parents that pressure their children to perform with this intensity?
- If you had a child who was a prodigy in some area, how would you handle it? Would you give up everything for that child to succeed, or insist that they put their talent in perspective and concentrate on being a child first and foremost?

Adults often give up their entire life, including their family life, in order to succeed themselves. People called "workaholics" are usually praised and rewarded for the number of hours spent at work, even though their dedication at the office often reflects a lack of time and attention at home.

- On the continuum from a lazy loafer to an addicted workaholic, where do you fall? Are you closer to being lazy or to being addicted to work? Do you think you are right in the middle? What do you think others would say? What would your friends and family say?
- Do you like where you fall on that continuum, or do you wish you were someplace else?
- When it comes to your faith, where would you fall on such a continuum? Are you lazy about your relationship to God? Are you so involved

with social, business, and church activities that your family is neglected? Or are you someplace in the healthy middle? Why do you think so?

For Teenagers

Building a tower takes a lot of planning, a lot of money, and a lot of labor. So do other things.
- Have you ever had a dream about accomplishing something—a dream that had you planning, thinking, and working in order to make it come true; a dream that you devoted lots of time and energy to? What is that dream? Are you still working on it? Or have you abandoned it?

Some young people throw themselves into a sport, a hobby, a talent, or an interest. They become known for their accomplishments in that area.
- What young person of your age do you know to be a very talented dancer? musician? artist? athlete? debater? writer?
- How much energy and dedication do these people invest in developing their skill?
- Into what area do you put the most time, energy, and enthusiasm? How successful or accomplished do you feel?
- How much time, energy, and enthusiasm do you invest in your relationship with God? in your involvement with your parish? in your relationships with your family? How can you give more of yourself to these areas?

For Children

Jesus says it's hard work to build a tower. You need supplies, you need a good plan, and you need people to help you. But people who care about getting the tower built can figure out how to do it.
- If you could build a giant tower in your backyard, what would you use to make it? Where would you put it? Who would you get to help you? Would your parent let you? Why or why not?

Jesus says it's hard work to make the world a better place, too. You need a good plan, you need people to help, and sometimes you need some supplies.

- If Jesus asked you to help make the world a better place in any way you wanted, what would you want to do? What would be your plan? Which people would you ask to help you? What supplies would you need?

Closing

At the root of human responsibility is the concept of perfection, the urge to achieve it, the intelligence to find a path towards it, and the will to follow that path, if not to the end at least the distance needed to rise above individual limitations and environmental impediments. —Aung San Suu Kyi

(Go for the Gold)

Twenty-Fourth Sunday of the Year

13 September 1998
16 September 2001
12 September 2004

Searching for a Lost Coin

Scripture

- *Exodus 32:7–11,13–14.* God's people are sinning against the commandments, but Moses begs that they not be punished, and so God forgives them.
- *1 Timothy 1:12–17.* In a letter to Timothy, Paul talks about what a sinner he had been, and how God had dealt with him so mercifully.
- *Luke 15:1–32.* When accused of eating with sinners, Jesus tells the parable of the lost sheep, the lost coin, and the lost prodigal.

Theme

No one is unimportant. God cares about everyone. God does not abandon the sinning Israelites; Paul is given grace and mercy; and God will chase after us with love like that of a shepherd who goes after a lost sheep, a loving parent who goes after a lost child, and a woman who goes after a lost coin in her home.

Focusing Object

Ten dimes or nickels, or nine coins plus one hidden in the room

Reflections

Like a shepherd who leaves ninety-nine relatively secure sheep to find the one missing sheep who has wandered away, God searches for sinners.

The story about the woman losing her one coin and cleaning the entire house until she finds it is probably the parable we can most relate to—most of us have more coins than sheep, and all of us know what it's like to lose something and to go out of our mind trying to locate it.

- If you had ten silver pieces and one was missing, how much time would you spend looking for that one piece?
- What is the most valuable item you have lost and then later found? How did you find it? Did you celebrate in any way after you found it?
- What is the most valuable item you have lost and never have found? Do you think you ever will? Why or why not?

God is just like that woman—searching for something precious that has been lost.

- Have you ever felt separated from God, or lost? Did you feel that God was trying to reconnect? What happened in your life to bring you back to God?
- Have you ever "lost" a relationship? Is there anyone in your life whom you love, but who is not on good terms with you now? What went wrong to cause this problem? How have you attempted to reconnect? What do you think might happen with this relationship in the future?

The woman searching for the lost coin is an image of God—the One who loves us, sees us as precious, knows we are lost, and searches for us until we are found.

- When have you felt "lost"? When have you felt far away from God? Do you feel that way now? If so, what is it like? How does it affect your life? If not, what happened to bring you back to God?

The woman searching for the lost coin can also be an image of us—one who sees a friend who is in trouble, or lost, who knows that the friend is precious, and who goes after that friend in the hope of being supportive until that friend can come around.

- When have you been that kind of support for a friend or a family member? What happened?

The woman searching for the lost coin can also be an image of a friend or parent searching for us when we are in a "lost" period of our life.

Lots of problems can bring us down so that we become depressed; develop unhealthy attitudes, behaviors, or addictions; and start to mess up our life.

- When have you needed some kind of special help or support during a "lost" time in your life? When you were the lost coin, who searched high and low looking for you, trying to bring you back?

The woman in the parable looked diligently until she found that lost coin.

- If you had ten silver pieces and one was missing, how much time would you spend looking for that one piece?
- What was the most valuable item you have ever lost? How long did you search for it? Did you ever find it? What did you do to celebrate?

For Children

God is like a wonderful woman who has ten important coins, but loses one, and then spends the whole day looking all over the house until she finds that coin.

Jesus says we are like the coins in his story. When we sin we are like the lost coin. But God, like the woman, puts everything else aside and comes looking for us. If we are sorry for our sins, God brings us back and celebrates with the angels, because all of heaven will be happy! That's how much God loves us.

- Have you ever lost anything? Where did you look for it? Did you ever find it? Where was it hiding?
- Did you ever lose a friend because that person did something to hurt you? Did you try to get back together with that friend? If so, did getting back together with that friend make you want to have a party with all your friends to celebrate you and your friend getting back together again?

Closing

Faithfulness in little things is a big thing. —Saint John Chrysostom

(Action 2000: C Cycle)

Twenty-Fifth Sunday of the Year

20 September 1998
23 September 2001
19 September 2004

Choosing God or Money

Scripture

- *Amos 8:4–7.* Amos scolds the unjust merchants who trample upon and cheat the poor. He insists that their sin of greed will not be forgotten.
- *1 Timothy 2:1–8.* In a letter to Timothy, Paul urges that prayers be offered for kings and others in authority.
- *Luke 16:1–13.* Jesus teaches us that we cannot live our life for money if we wish to live our life for God.

Theme

Greed, dishonesty, and injustice abound in our world. Amos warns that greedy actions will be remembered. Jesus warns us to be trustworthy in small matters, so we might be trusted in larger matters. And in the midst of this problematic and imperfect world, Paul asks us to pray for the people who govern us.

Focusing Object
A dollar bill

Reflections

Jesus tells an interesting story to lead up to his warning about greed, or love for money. A rich man fires his manager, and that manager makes allies among his customers by reducing the amount of their debt to the rich man. Rather than being angry, the rich man liked this manager's shrewdness. It takes one to know one!

Obviously Jesus does not want us to be dishonest, but he does want us to be resourceful. If we served the Reign of God with as much savvy as this manager served himself, think of what might happen.

- Friendships can be political. Jesus knows that. What is he telling us about the friendships we form and the way trust can affect relationships?
- How does greed or love for money get in the way of serving God? Is there money you do not need to spend on yourself that might be used in a less selfish way? What might you do with that amount of money?

Jesus tells us that trust is based on performance. If you have shown yourself to be responsible in small things, then you will be trusted with larger things. If you have shown yourself to be careless or dishonest, even in a small matter, you will not be trusted in a more important matter.

- Do these words ring true? How does your trust level—high or low—affect your relationships?
- When has your "track record" with your parents or teachers come back to haunt you? When have you lost trust, and then lost an opportunity for something you wanted?
- When has your track record with your parents or teachers helped you? When have you proven yourself to be responsible so that you earned a privilege you wanted?

Jesus warns us that we cannot be a slave to two masters—God and money. We must decide which is more important, and then live our life accordingly.

- Do you think that Jesus is implying that you can't have any money? Or do you think Jesus is concerned only with an excess of money, a preoccupation with material things, and the greed that makes us jealous or dissatisfied with what we have?
- If Jesus were to rate most teenagers based on excess of money, preoccupation with material things, and a tendency toward greed, jealousy, and dissatisfaction, how well would most teenagers do? How well would you do?
- Why is money such a problem? Why is greed so common? How do people learn to become so selfish?

For Children

Jesus warns us that if we care too much about money and things, then we won't worry enough about God and people.

- What do you think most people like better—money or God? Why do you think that? Do you think the choice most people make is a good one?
- What makes you the most happy—being with people who love you and care about you, or having a lot of nice things? Why?
- If you had a lot of money and could use it in any way you wanted in order to help other people, what would you do with the money?

Closing

There must be more to life than having everything! —Maurice Sendak

(Random Acts of Kindness)

Twenty-Sixth Sunday of the Year

27 September 1998
30 September 2001
26 September 2004

Lazarus and the Rich Man

Scripture

- *Amos 6:1,4–7.* Amos attacks the rich and their indulgent lifestyles. The distress of the poor doesn't bother these rich people.
- *1 Timothy 6:11–16.* Paul reminds Timothy that God alone is the One to focus on, the One to value above everything else.
- *Luke 16:19–31.* Jesus tells the story of Lazarus, who was poor while on earth, yet became rich in heaven.

Theme

Jesus and Amos probably would not have any trouble with people being so very rich, as long as there were not any people who were so very poor. But when the needs of the very poor are ignored or caused by the very rich, it is very troubling indeed. Because this rich man in the Gospel valued money over service, he ended up paying for his greed in the eternal fires. Paul's message for us is to remember to value God over everything, including money.

Focusing Object
A dish of crumbs

Reflections

For Adults

This rich man does not seem to mind having a diseased, homeless man lying at his gate. He feasts right in front of Lazarus, unmindful that just his table scraps would be enough to satisfy the poor man's hunger.

- What do you do with your table scraps? Do you waste food and throw it away? Or do you pay attention to the amount of food you buy and eat so that it is not wasted?
- When you eat out in a restaurant, if you have food left over, do you take it home to eat later or do you let it be thrown away?
- What do your habits with food say about how highly you value food? Do your food habits encourage others to be less wasteful or more wasteful?
- How do your own personal food habits affect your attitude about world poverty and hunger? Do you find yourself contributing to food pantries, serving in food kitchens, and participating in walks and drives to raise money and food for poor people? If so, what is that involvement like? If not, what stands in the way of some kind of involvement?
- The Gospel teaches that those who are rich in this life will be suffering in the next, and that those who suffer in this life will be rich in the next. How is your life different when you take that message seriously?

For Teenagers

This story has two characters, and only one of the characters has a name. Usually, the main character of a story—the important one—is the one named, since being known by a name signifies status. But in this story, it is the poor man who has a name—Lazarus. The rich man remains nameless.

- If the story ended when these two people died, what would you think of the status of Lazarus and the status of the rich man? Who would have seemed the more significant character? Why?

- In the afterlife the rich man knows Lazarus by name. Do you think this means he might have known Lazarus by name while he was alive? If so, what kind of relationship do you think they had?
- The rich man allowed Lazarus to remain by his gate. Would you feel comfortable with a homeless, diseased man living in your backyard? Was the rich man more or less tolerant and compassionate than you might be? How does that affect you?

We are a very wasteful society. Some have estimated that 50 percent or more of the food at restaurants is thrown out. Lots of hungry, homeless people could be fed with that amount of table scraps.

- Do you ever waste food? Are you more likely to throw food out if you are alone or if you are with your friends? What difference does it make, either way?
- Are there any opportunities for you to serve the needs of the hungry, such as in a food pantry or soup kitchen? What does your own church do for the poor and hungry? Would you like to become involved in some way? Why or why not?

For Children

Jesus tells a story about two people: a man who was very rich and a man named Lazarus who was poor and hungry. Lazarus often watched the rich man eat, and longed for just the crumbs that were left over. But the rich man, even though he had a lot of food, didn't give him any—not even the crumbs.

- Which man do you think Jesus liked better— Lazarus or the rich man? Why?
- How hungry would you be if you only got to eat the crumbs that were left over from somebody else's supper?
- If you were Lazarus and you were hungry, and you saw the crumbs on the rich man's plate every day, what would you say? What would you do?

- If you were the rich man, and you saw poor, hungry Lazarus watching you eat day after day, what would you do? Would you give him your dish of leftover crumbs? Or would you invite him to eat supper with you? Why?

Closing

With money, a dragon. Without money, a worm.
—A Chinese proverb

(Acts of Faith)

Twenty-Seventh Sunday of the Year

4 October 1998
7 October 2001
3 October 2004

Moving Trees with Mustard-Seed-Sized Faith

Scripture

- *Habakkuk 1:2–3; 2:2–4.* The prophet Habakkuk cries out to God about the violence and strife all around him. God assures him that the time ending all this will come. Only patience and faith can help Habakkuk endure.
- *2 Timothy 1:6–8,13–14.* Paul advises Timothy to bear all hardships with the faith that comes from the Holy Spirit.
- *Luke 17:5–10.* The Apostles ask Jesus to increase their faith, and Jesus replies that if they had faith the size of a tiny mustard seed they could command giant trees to be uprooted and transplanted into the sea.

Theme

This is a very common theme throughout all the Scriptures—requests for more faith, and help to endure suffering. God is comforting Habakkuk, Paul is comforting Timothy, and Jesus is comforting the Apostles. Where is the source of this faith and comfort we seek? The Holy Spirit.

Focusing Object

A seed

Reflections

Faith and comfort—everyone seems to always be looking for more faith and comfort. Jesus makes it seem so easy. The amount of faith the size of a seed could move a tree! If that is so, then what is the amount of faith we have—we who can barely move ourselves to action?

- Do you consider yourself to be a person of great faith? Why or why not?
- Have you ever received great comfort from someone at a time of great suffering? What did that person say or do to help you?
- Who is a person of great faith that you know? What have you noticed about that person that reveals his or her faith?
- If you had stronger faith, how do you think your life would be different? What can you do to help increase your faith?

Jesus is telling the Apostles how small their faith actually is. If their faith were bigger—as big as the size of a tiny seed, for example—they could command trees to fly through the air and land in the sea! So obviously he must consider their faith to be very small indeed.

- How about your faith? Do you think it is large or small? Why?
- What influences affect your faith? Has any life experience of yours increased your faith? What happened?
- Has any life experience hurt your faith and caused you to have doubts about God? What happened?

Not only does Jesus expect the Apostles to do great things with their faith, but to also see these miracles as "no big deal"—as if they were to say: "It was nothing. We were just doing our job."

- Have you ever done anything that impressed someone else, yet you yourself didn't think it was such a big deal? What was it that you did?

- Have you ever seen someone do something that impressed you, yet to that person it was no big deal? What did that person do?
- Do you believe that having more faith—in God, in yourself, in the power that comes from the Holy Spirit—could really cause miracles to occur? Why or why not?

For Children

Jesus wants us to have faith that good things can happen. When people don't believe in Jesus, they can feel sad and lonely. Knowing about Jesus can help people feel better and do more. That way, good things can happen.

Jesus said all we need is faith this big—the size of a tiny seed. That doesn't look like much faith, but Jesus thinks that would be plenty.

- How much do you believe in Jesus? A whole lot—a big amount? Or just a little bit?
- What do you believe about Jesus? What is Jesus like? What do you think he would say about your day today?
- What good things do you think can happen in your life today? What about this week or this month? What good things do you think will happen before the end of the year?

Closing

If you think you can, you can. And if you think you can't, you're right. —Mary Kay Ash

(Success Every Day)

Twenty-Eighth Sunday of the Year

11 October 1998
14 October 2001
10 October 2004

The One
Who Said
"Thank-You"

Scripture

- *2 Kings 5:14–17.* Naaman was cleaned of his leprosy when he did what Elisha told him to do: plunge into the Jordan River seven times.
- *2 Timothy 2:8–13.* Paul has us remember that Jesus rose from the dead, so that if we die with Jesus, we will also rise with Jesus.
- *Luke 17:11–19.* Jesus cures ten people of leprosy, and only one returns to thank him for the healing. The one who returns is a Samaritan.

Theme

Believing in Jesus is believing in life after death, and in joy after sorrow. Naaman did not really think he would be cured by going into the Jordan River; in fact, he almost did not even try. But once he did, his conversion was so great that he wanted to bring back some of the sacred earth from the holy place of the one true God. He was thankful. On the other hand, most of the lepers in this Gospel were less thankful, even though they seemed to have no doubts that they could be cured.

Focusing Object
A thank-you card

Reflections

Naaman did not have high expectations. He almost dismissed the healing advice Elisha gave to him. And his response after being cured was pure awe and gratitude. He tried to give Elisha a gift, but Elisha would not accept it. Doing God's work is gift enough.

- When you're not expecting much, are you more thankful for blessings?
- When was a time that you were surprised with an unexpected blessing? What was your response?

The lepers that met Jesus called him by name and begged for his pity. They probably would not have bothered if they didn't think Jesus had the power to cure them. If the only one who returned to thank Jesus was a Samaritan, a person Jews were taught to regard as less worthy than themselves, one wonders if the other nine were Jews. One could further wonder if the other nine thought themselves better than that one Samaritan, and therefore, being Jews, thought they *deserved* a cure more than that Samaritan did. Perhaps they might have even been angry that the Samaritan was treated just as well as the rest of them. There is no evidence to support such a theory, but one can wonder.

- When you are expecting something, are you less thankful when it comes?
- If you think yourself more deserving of an honor or compliment than another person, yet both you and this other person receive the same honor or compliment, does that taint your feeling of gratitude? Has such a thing ever happened to you?
- Why do the blessings of others sometimes have a negative impact on the thankfulness we feel about our own blessings?

For Teenagers

Ten lepers are cured of a disgusting and horrible disease, yet only one returns to say thank-you to Jesus. If they were asked, it's possible these nine lepers who chose not to express their gratitude to

Jesus all had some reason or excuse. Perhaps they forgot or were too tired or couldn't find their way back.

- Can you think of nine different reasons why people don't thank others who have done them a kind service?
- How are you with saying thank-you? How are you with writing thank-you notes? How are you with feeling lucky and thankful for all your blessings?

A common saying is that we only appreciate something when we don't have it or when it's not working right or when it hurts or is broken.

- How often do you think about your legs or your eyes or your ears? Does your awareness of their role in your life increase after you spend time with a person who is deaf or blind, or who uses a wheelchair? Why is that?
- How often do you appreciate electricity? or plumbing? or automobiles? What would your life be like without these conveniences?

For Children

Jesus met ten people who were very sick. Jesus healed them and made them all better. But only one of those ten said thank-you. Jesus never saw the other nine again.

- Do you think Jesus felt hurt when only one person said thank-you? Why or why not?
- What do you think those other nine people were thinking about? Why do you think they forgot to say thank-you to Jesus?
- Did you ever receive something special or get to do something special, but then forgot to say thank-you? What happened?

Closing

When the shoe fits, we forget about the feet.
—*The Wisdom of the Taoists*

(Acts of Faith)

Twenty-Ninth Sunday of the Year

18 October 1998
21 October 2001
17 October 2004

The Persistent Widow

Scripture

- *Exodus 17:8–13.* As long as Moses kept his arms up, Joshua remained victorious in battle. When Moses could no longer persist on his own, Aaron and Hur held up Moses' arms for him.
- *2 Timothy 3:14—4:2.* Paul challenges Timothy to not lose patience, and to stay with his task of preaching the word, remembering who his teachers were.
- *Luke 18:1–8.* In a parable Jesus praises the determination of a widow who is finally given justice, even by a corrupt judge, because she was tenacious. Her persistence wore the judge out. That is how we need to be.

Theme

Don't give up. Be persistent. Be tenacious. Be determined. Persevere. Don't lose patience. Keep going. This is a consistent message coming to us from Moses, Paul, and Jesus. It is especially true of our prayer life. Jesus promises that God will answer prayers and bring justice—but will people believe and patiently persevere?

Focusing Object

A clock or a watch

Reflections

For Adults

When things take so much time, it is easy to run out of patience. Often we are tempted to give up and stop trying.

- What is an accomplishment that took you a lot of time and persistence, but that was finally successful? How did you keep believing in yourself during the process? Did you ever lose faith?
- What is something you did give up on? Was it truly time to let it go? Or do you sometimes have regrets and wish you had been more persistent?

Jesus tells us the story of the tenacious widow as a parable about prayer. Many people have a hard time praying, saying that it does nothing for them and that they feel as if they are talking to a wall and not being heard. But many other people would offer the insight that the purpose of prayer is not for us to change God, but for God to change us. If so, being persistent will give us extra time to be changed.

- Is your prayer life active and fulfilling? Do you feel connected with God? Or do you feel like giving up since "nothing is happening"?
- What might help you become more like that tenacious widow with your prayer life? What might help "something happen"?

For Teenagers

Think of any successful scientist, any successful musician, any successful writer. None of these people became successful overnight. It usually takes a lot of time and a lot of mistakes—*a lot of close attempts*—before success comes. That's true in any area of life.

If you learn from every mistake you make, then nothing you do can ever be seen as a failure. Every mistake can become a valuable lesson and an important step on the way to where you want to go.

- What is a mistake you made that actually taught you something important?
- Do you give up easily? Do you think you are a "quitter"? Why or why not?

- Are you too persistent? Are you too tenacious? Do you sometimes need help to realize when it's time to "let it go and get on with your life"? Why do you think so?
- When has persistence paid off for you?

Jesus advises us to be persistent in prayer. Prayer is our communication with God, our relationship with the Divine. Like any friendship, a prayer relationship takes time, effort, and energy.

- How do you keep your friendships with others fresh and fulfilling? How do you keep your friendship with God fresh and fulfilling? Do you use the same techniques for both friendships? Why or why not?

For Children

Jesus tells us a story about a woman who needed something, and a man who had what she needed but didn't care very much about her. He could have helped her, but he kept telling her no. But this woman kept telling him over and over what she needed, until the man who didn't care finally said yes. He didn't say yes because he cared about her, but he said yes because he got tired of hearing her tell him the same thing over and over. It took her a long time to get what she needed, but it happened.

The world has a lot of problems. Some people aren't very nice. They steal things and destroy things, and some people hurt other people with guns. But a lot of nice people live in our world, too.

- What do you think would happen if all the nice people kept doing nice things, over and over and over? Do you think the stealing and destroying and hurting would finally stop? Would it take a long time? Why or why not?

Jesus says it's a good idea to pray over and over and over for the world to be a better place. Jesus says we need to pray every day and to not give up.

- Do you pray every day? What do you pray for? How do you want the world to become better? Do you think it will take a long time for that to happen? Why or why not?

Closing

Let me tell you the secret that has led me to my goal. My strength lies solely in my tenacity.
—Louis Pasteur

(Success Every Day)

Thirtieth Sunday of the Year

25 October 1998
28 October 2001
24 October 2004

The Proud Pharisee and the Humble Sinner

Scripture

- *Sirach 35:12–14,16–18.* Sirach reminds us that God always hears the prayer of the poor, the oppressed, and the weak.
- *2 Timothy 4:6–8,16–18.* Paul reviews his life, telling Timothy that although he had been abandoned by many, still he fought the good fight, ran the good race, and is ready to be with Jesus.
- *Luke 18:9–14.* Jesus tells the parable about the proud Pharisee and the humble sinner who both went to the temple to pray.

Theme

The prayer of the lowly is always heard. Proud prayers, however, are not as effective. Every sinner can take comfort knowing that sincere and simple prayers are heard despite the sins of a past life. Paul knows this. He is all alone, exhausted by life, and he writes from prison, looking back at all he has been through, still confident that Jesus will be there for him.

Focusing Object
Salt and pepper shakers

Reflections

For Adults

Some people see salt and pepper as opposites, yet others see them as complements. Many opposites can also be seen as complements, in context. Like pride and humility: they seem like opposites, but each has a healthy place in a person with good self-esteem.

- What are you proud of? What do you know you are good at?
- What are you humbled by? What places, things, problems, or jobs simply overwhelm you?

Jesus contrasts the proud prayer of a Pharisee, who sees himself as better than others, with the humble prayer of an honest person, who sees sinfulness as something to seek forgiveness for. And clearly, it is the humble one who is closer to God.

- Is it possible to become too proud and too full of yourself? Why? When have you come close to being this way? What helped you regain your perspective?
- Is it also possible to become too ashamed about yourself? Why? When have you come close to being this way? What helped you regain your perspective?
- How can we find a balance between pride and humility in a way that Jesus would accept and approve?

For Teenagers

Some people like just salt on their food and other people like only pepper. Like black and white, salt and pepper seem to be opposites. But some people like them both and use them together, as complements to each other's flavor. The proud Pharisee and the humble sinner seem to be opposites, but they can also be seen as complements as well.

The proud Pharisee was able to understand the good things about himself. This gave him confidence to pray in thanksgiving for his blessings.

- It's good to be thankful for blessings, but Jesus would probably say the proud Pharisee took it a bit too far. Why do you think so?

The humble sinner was able to understand the flaws in himself. But still he had the confidence to pray for forgiveness and mercy. It's good to be aware of all your flaws, but a person could take this a bit too far as well.

- Do you think Jesus wants us to focus only on our sinfulness, and to be obsessed with being an unworthy, "second-class" citizen? Why or why not?
- Is it possible to have a healthy pride in your talents, as well as a healthy humility in your place on earth as a servant of God? What would that look like? How would you know when you had achieved such a balance?
- By the way, which do you like better—salt or pepper? Or do you like them both? Do you see them as opposites or complements? black and white or shades of gray?

For Children

Jesus tells a story about two people that are different—different like salt and pepper are different. One of these people liked to brag about how important he was and how terrible another person was. The other person didn't brag at all. Jesus wants us to be like the person who doesn't brag.

- Why would Jesus not want us to brag? How would other people feel if they were to hear us bragging?
- How would you feel if someone else was telling you that they were more special than you?
- Do you think that some people truly are better than others, or do you think that everyone is special in their own way? Why?
- Which do you like better—salt or pepper? Or do you like both?

Closing

Most people enjoy the inferiority of their friends; real friends don't notice it. —Norman Douglas

(Acts of Faith)

Thirty-First Sunday of the Year

The readings for this Sunday do not occur in 1998.
4 November 2001
31 October 2004

Zacchaeus

Scripture

- *Wisdom 11:22—12:1.* God made the whole world, and God loves all of us, even forgiving us when we sin.
- *2 Thessalonians 1:11—2:2.* May God make you worthy of what you are called to do, so God's name might be glorified.
- *Luke 19:1–10.* Jesus calls Zacchaeus down from a tree so they can dine together. Zacchaeus, a tax collector, proclaims a promise to be fair and honest in his work.

Theme

God created us, God calls us forth to be our best, and God loves us, even when we sin. Like Zacchaeus, we can begin again and keep our promise to do better. We are always forgiven.

Focusing Object

A tree

Reflections

For Adults

Zacchaeus obviously wanted to see Jesus, because he climbed a tree in order to see better. Jesus must have recognized his determination, because he picked him out right away, much to the disappointment of the crowd who regarded Zacchaeus as a sinner.

- Sometimes we know we need help with something, so we put ourselves in the position of being noticed. It is more subtle and safer than asking outright. When have you wanted someone to help you with something, but instead of asking directly, you either dropped hints or you allowed the other person to observe or learn about your situation? Did it work? Did you get the help you wanted, or did you then have to try a more direct approach?
- When has someone else given you a hint of needing help? Did you help? Or were you not observant enough to pick up on the hint?
- Which approach do you prefer—the direct approach of asking or being asked specifically? or the more subtle approach that requires one to take notice?

Zacchaeus was chosen by Jesus. He heard the crowd's accusations about him, assessed their truth, and proclaimed his intention to amend his ways. Jesus believed him and affirmed that salvation had come to his house. It was a moment of conversion for Zacchaeus and for the crowd. Zacchaeus learned he was worthy and so did everyone else.

- When was your "worth" affirmed or acknowledged by others? What were the circumstances, and what was that like for you?
- What "truth" is difficult for you to hear? How could you put the hearing of this truth into action in your daily life?

Zacchaeus probably didn't like crowds. He was short and needed to climb a tree in order to see Jesus better.

- Do you like crowds? Why or why not?
- What are some other reasons why some people might not like crowds?

- What are some reasons why some people might like crowds?

Zacchaeus seemed to know that he had been dishonest as a tax collector, yet he told the crowd right away that he was giving half of his money to the poor, and paying back four times as much money to anyone he had cheated. This was quite a generous offer.

- Have you ever wronged anyone and then had to figure out a way to make it up to that person? What did you do? How did it work out? Did a lot of people know about it? What was their reaction?
- Did anyone ever wrong you and then try to make it up to you? Were you forgiving or not? Why? Are you friends with this person now? Why or why not?

For Children

Zacchaeus wanted to see Jesus, but he was too short to see over all the people in the crowd. So he climbed a sycamore tree to get a better view.

- Have you ever climbed a tree? Did you ever have a tree house? If not, would you like to? Why or why not? Did you ever go into someone else's tree house? What is the view like from a tree?

Jesus saw Zacchaeus in the tree and told him to come down so Jesus could eat at his house. The other people said Zacchaeus was a sinner, but Zacchaeus said he wouldn't sin anymore, and Jesus knew Zacchaeus was telling the truth.

- Did you ever tell someone you weren't going to make a certain mistake any more? Did that person think you were telling the truth?
- What is a mistake you used to make, but you don't make anymore?

Closing

Spiritual growth results from absorbing and digesting truth and putting it to practice in daily life.
—White Eagle

(Acts of Faith)

Thirty-Second Sunday of the Year

8 November 1998
11 November 2001
7 November 2004

Make Progress, Speed On, and Triumph

Scripture

- *2 Maccabees 7:1–2,9–14.* Seven Jewish brothers and their mother, who were tortured and killed for remaining faithful to the Law, believed in life after death and found courage in that belief.
- ° *2 Thessalonians 2:16—3:5.* We are reminded to make progress and to remember that God will give us the strength and courage we need.
- *Luke 20:27–38.* The Sadducees, who did not believe in life after death, try to fool Jesus with a question about a woman who marries and then outlives each of seven brothers.

Theme

We are called to pray and work so that the word of Jesus makes progress. Our strength and courage for proclaiming the word comes from our belief in the Resurrection, and in our reward for every good work and good word. On this earth the seven murdered brothers and their mother looked foolish, but they believed God would surely restore them to life. They believed that God is not the God of the dead, but the God of the living.

Focusing Object

A toy racing car

Reflections

For Adults

We are urged to pray that the message of Jesus *makes progress*. This phrase, "makes progress," is translated many different ways in different Bibles. The New Jerusalem Bible says "spread quickly." The Good News Bible and the New Revised Standard Version say "spread rapidly." The Carmelite translation says "speed on and triumph." It is urgent that we race on and get this message of Jesus out to the world. That is quite a command.

- Do you see your task to get the message of Jesus out to the world as a serious command? Why or why not?
- How serious is this call to all Christians? How urgent a matter is it? Must it really be a top priority, or can we put it on the back burner for now?

We are urged to pray that we will be delivered from those who are evil and confused. We are told to find our strength and confidence in Jesus.

- Do you actually find strength and confidence in Jesus? Or is Jesus still sort of abstract to you?
- Who in your life might be evil or confused? Do you ever fall into that category yourself? How so?

For Teenagers

We are urged to pray that the message of Jesus *makes progress*. This phrase, "makes progress," is translated many different ways in different Bibles. The New Jerusalem Bible says "spread quickly." The Good News Bible and the New Revised Standard Version say "spread rapidly." The Carmelite translation says "speed on and triumph." It is urgent that we race on and get this message of Jesus out to everyone.

We are being told, "Hurry up! Get going! Get the message of Jesus out there! Get everyone talking about Jesus! Don't waste any more time! This is important stuff! High priority!"

- What is the message of Jesus? How would you explain it to someone?

- Do you live your life with this urgency to get out the message of Jesus? Why or why not?
- What is the most pressing matter in your life right now? What is your most urgent need or issue? Where does the message of Jesus fit in with all this?

For Children

We are being asked to do some important work for Jesus. We are being asked to hurry up and help more people understand what Jesus wants us to do. We aren't supposed to be lazy about this. We are supposed to get going fast—like a racing car—and start living and talking and acting in a way that shows everyone what Jesus wants.

- What do you think Jesus wants us to do?
- What are some things you can do that will show others what Jesus wants the world to be like?
- Do you like racing cars? Can they get you places fast? Can a racing car help us to do Jesus' work any faster? Why or why not?
- Why are we supposed to be fast like a racing car when it comes to doing what Jesus wants?

Closing

It is better to wear out than to rust out. —Bishop Richard Cumberland

(Success Every Day)

Thirty-Third Sunday of the Year

15 November 1998
18 November 2001
14 November 2004

The Day Will Come

Scripture

- *Malachi 3:19–20.* Lo, the day is coming when the evil ones will be set on fire, and the faithful followers will see the sun of justice rise up.
- *2 Thessalonians 3:7–12.* Some members of the early church thought the end of the world was coming soon, that there was no need to do any work. Paul laid down the rule: If you do not work, you will not eat.
- *Luke 21:5–19.* Jesus describes the coming of the day when not one stone will be left upon another. There will be earthquakes and famines, persecution and trials, but patient endurance will save us.

Theme

The end of the world is a popular thing to discuss—in our day (especially as we come to the end of a millennium), in the time of the Christian Testament, and in the time of the Hebrew Scriptures. Lo, the day is coming when justice will be done, when one stone will not be left upon another. But it probably won't be tomorrow, so let's not quit our jobs to stay home and wait it out. And when it does come, although it will be filled with catastrophe, ultimately we will all be saved.

Focusing Object

Two stones

Reflections

For Adults

End-of-the-world descriptions are always exciting, mysterious, and intriguing: lots of images of destruction and fire and signs in the sky; not one stone will be left upon another.

- Have you ever worried about the end of the world? Why or why not?
- Have you ever tried to imagine it? What does your mental picture of it look like?
- A common response to doomsday predictions is to not worry about how the world might die, but instead how the world might live. Does this shift in perspective change the way you feel about these Scriptures?

When "that day" comes, Jesus tells us that some of us will be put to death. But his next sentence also says that not a hair of our head will be harmed.

- Do you have trouble reconciling these two juxtaposed contradictions? How can this make sense?
- How much fear do you have regarding the final judgment?
- How much faith and confidence do you have in God's promise of protection?

For Teenagers

Every so often, some famous person or group comes along to predict the exact day of the end of the world. Everyone gets excited, lots of news coverage is aired, and a lot of conversation is stirred up. Why not? It's an exciting possibility. People like talking about it: What might it be like? How will we know if it's coming? Is it possible to read the signs? Will it happen while we are still alive?

- Do such questions and conversations bore you or interest you? Do they cause you any concern? How so?
- Have you heard any specific predictions lately about the end of the world? Do you put much stock in such predictions? Why or why not?

Very often, when people get nervous about "the end of the world," it's because there is a lot of fear of death and final judgment. But actually, the odds are not very high that tomorrow will be the last day of the world. The odds, however, are very high that tomorrow will be the last day of *someone's* life. That's because many people die every day. We never know when it will be our turn. When it happens to someone we love, it is tragic, and often sudden and shocking even though we know that, sooner or later, it happens to us all.

Instead of worrying about living the last day of the world, why not begin to appreciate life and those we love as if every day could be our last? (or their last?)

- How is your life different when you try to do that? How would your life be different if everyone tried to do that?

For Children

Some people were looking at the Temple and all the beautiful stones it was made of. Jesus reminded them that things—even beautiful things—don't last forever. If we love things too much, we will be in trouble, because sooner or later all things get destroyed. And the day will come when not one stone of that beautiful temple will be left on top of another. Things break.

Jesus wants us to love people more than things. Jesus wants us to know that when things break apart, they are destroyed and ruined. But when people die, they are not destroyed. They go to heaven to live with Jesus forever.

- Is there anything that you once had that now is broken? What was it? How did it break?
- Do you know anyone who has died? Do you miss them? What do you think life is like for them now, in heaven?

Closing

You don't get to choose how you're going to die, or when. You can only decide how you're going to live. Now. —Joan Baez

(The Promise of a New Day)

Thirty-Fourth Sunday of the Year (Christ the King)

22 November 1998
25 November 2001
21 November 2004

 King
of the Jews

Scripture

- *2 Samuel 5:1–3.* David is anointed the king of Israel.
- *Colossians 1:12–20.* Through Jesus we have forgiveness of sins. We were rescued from the darkness and brought into his kingdom.
- ° *Luke 23:35–43.* Hanging under the sign that declares him to be the King of the Jews, Jesus forgives the criminal who repents. They would see each other in paradise before the end of that day.

Theme

Jesus is descended from David, the king of Israel, yet he is a king of another kind, ruling over life and death, freeing us from sin and darkness. Working for the kingdom of Jesus is working for understanding and forgiveness in this world, and paradise in the next.

Focusing Object
A crucifix or the letters *INRI*

Reflections

For Adults

To imagine the fear and pain of such a vicious and physically torturous death as crucifixion is difficult. Of the two criminals, one joined the crowd, screaming at Jesus and demanding that he save all of them if he was indeed the Messiah. The other one called Jesus by name and asked to be remembered.

- When you are faced with pain and fear, what do you do? How do you respond? Do you scream and cry and lash out at someone nearby? Do you calmly endure? Or do you react in all these ways? Jesus rules over life and death. Sometimes that can be more frightening than comforting.
- If Jesus can forgive a thief, is there any sin he will not forgive us for if we repent? After all, how many of us are criminals?
- On the other hand, that thief seemed to be re-markable—rebuking the other one's mockery and calmly asking for forgiveness in the midst of such agony. When have you responded with such clarity in the midst of a difficult situation?

For Teenagers

What do you know about kings? Kings have power and authority. They live in palaces, with good food, entertainment, and servants.

- How is this image similar to your idea of who Jesus is? How is this image different?
- Do you think Jesus made a big deal about being a "king" when he was hanging out with the Apostles? How do you think he treated them?

Lots of people wonder what "INRI" stands for. Think of each *"I"* as a *"J,"* and it's easier to see. *J*esus of *N*azareth, King (*"R*ex" in Latin) of the *J*ews. Jesus wasn't in the habit of calling himself King of the Jews.

- How do you think he got that title? Who would have most likely seen him as a real king and lead-er? Why? Who might have used that title only in a mocking way? Why?
- If Jesus came today instead of two thousand years ago, do you think modern Americans would see him as a king? Why or why not?
- Do you see Jesus as a king? If not, why not? If so, a king of what? or a king of whom?

For Children

- One of Jesus' names is "Christ the King." Have you ever read a story about a king? What are kings like?
- How is Jesus like a king?
- Kings live in a kingdom, and they take care of the people that live in their kingdom. How does Jesus take care of us?
- Jesus was crucified with two criminals. One of the criminals made fun of Jesus, and the other one asked Jesus to forgive him for his sins. Jesus did. Which criminal understood who Jesus was? Why do you think so?

Closing

There is nothing wrong in admitting you are afraid. But whenever something threatens you, instead of running away, hold your ground and repeat the mantra "Rama, Rama" (God, God) over and over again in your mind. It can turn your fear into fearlessness. —Advice of an old family servant to Mohandas K. Gandhi

(Go for the Gold)

Index by Theme

Index by Focusing Object

Acknowledgments *(continued)*

The excerpts on pages 18, 37, 80, and 94 are from *Action 2000: Praying Scripture in a Contemporary Way: C Cycle,* by Mark Link, SJ (Allen, TX: Tabor Publishing, 1992), pages 298, 30, 280, and 160, respectively. Copyright © 1992 by Mark Link.

The excerpts on pages 21 30, 40, 43, 55, 61, 64, 73, 101, 107, 114, and 117 are taken from *Acts of Faith: Daily Meditations for People of Color,* by Iyanla Vanzant (New York: Simon and Schuster, Fireside Book, 1993), n.p. Copyright © 1993 by Iyanla Vanzant.

The excerpts on pages 25, 46, 58, and 67 (adapted) are from *The Road Less Traveled,* by M. Scott Peck, MD (New York: Simon and Schuster, Touchstone Book, 1978), pages 168, 150, 107, and 130, respectively. Copyright © 1978 by M. Scott Peck.

The excerpts on pages 28, 49, and 123 are from *The Promise of a New Day,* by Karen Casey and Martha Vanceburg (New York: HarperCollins Publishers, Hazelden Book, 1983), n.p. Copyright © 1983 by the Hazelden Foundation.

The excerpt on page 34 is from *Familiar Quotations by John Bartlett,* edited by Emily Morison Beck (Boston: Little, Brown and Company, 1968), page 789. Copyright © 1968 by Little, Brown and Company.

The excerpts on pages 70, 104, 111, and 120 are from *Success Every Day,* by Weight Watchers (New York: Macmillan General Reference, 1996), n.p. Copyright © 1996 by Weight Watchers International.

The excerpt on page 76 is from *Vision 2000: Praying Scripture in a Contemporary Way: A Cycle,* by Mark Link, SJ (Allen, TX: Tabor Publishing, 1992), page 96. Copyright © 1992 by Mark Link.

The excerpts on pages 86, 90, and 126 are from *Go for the Gold: Thoughts on Achieving Your Personal Best* (Kansas City, MO: Andrews and McMeel, 1995), pages 256, 89, and 152, respectively. Copyright © 1995 by Armand Eisen.

The excerpt on page 97 is from *Random Acts of Kindness,* by the editors of Conari Press (Berkeley, CA: Conari Press, 1993), page 114. Copyright © 1993 by Conari Press.

"One of the unique characteristics of this book, along with reflections on the lectionary readings, is the inclusion of a focusing object. Besides lending insights into the Scriptures, the focusing object trains people to see symbolically. In doing so, it enhances the ability 'to see more than meets the eye,' to see the extraordinary in the ordinary, the sacred in the secular." **Dr. Maureen Gallagher**, Archbishop's Delegate for Parishes, Diocese of Milwaukee, Wisconsin

"Lisa-Marie is definitely 'in touch' with the needs of young people and families—and how they approach the word of God. *In Touch with the Word* will not only help various generations in praying the Scriptures, but will also assist homilists in making the word come alive in their preaching." **Thomas N. Tomaszek, MEd, MTS**, Director, Spectrum Resources, Milwaukee, Wisconsin, and consultant to the National Federation for Catholic Youth Ministry's Prayer and Worship Project Team